COLLECTOR'S
VALUE GUIDE™

Ty® Plush Animals

Collector Handbook and Price Guide

THIRD EDITION

Ty® Plush Animals

Front cover (left to right): "Peter™" *(Attic Treasures™);* "Monkeybaby™" *(Baby Ty™);* "Bushy™" *(Beanie Babies®);* "Paddles™" *(Pillow Pals®);* "Claude™" *(Teenie Beanie Babies™);* "Cromwell™" *(Attic Treasures™);* "2000 Signature Bear™" *(Beanie Buddies®);* "Angel™" *(Beanie Kids™).*

Back cover (top to bottom): "Lucky™" *(Beanie Babies®);* "Elmer™" *(Ty Classic™);* "Rascal™" *(Beanie Kids™).*

Managing Editor:	Jeff Mahony	Creative Director:	Joe T. Nguyen
Associate Editors:	Melissa A. Bennett	Production Supervisor:	Scott Sierakowski
	Jan Cronan	Senior Graphic Designers:	Lance Doyle
	Gia C. Manalio		Susannah C. Judd
	Paula Stuckart		David S. Maloney
Contributing Editor:	Mike Micciulla		Carole Mattia-Slater
Editorial Assistants:	Timothy R. Affleck	Graphic Designers:	Jennifer J. Bennett
	Heather N. Carreiro		Sean-Ryan Dudley
	Jennifer Filipek		Kimberly Eastman
	Beth Hackett		Marla B. Gladstone
	Nicole LeGard Lenderking		Robert Kyerematen
	Steven Shinkaruk		Angi Shearstone
	Joan C. Wheal		David Ten Eyck
Web Reporter:	Samantha Bouffard	Art Interns:	Huy Hoang
			Anna Zagajewska
		Web Graphic Designer:	Ryan Falis
		Product Development	
		Manager:	Paul Rasid
		R&D Specialist:	Priscilla Berthiaume

ISBN 1-888914-86-6

CheckerBee
PUBLISHING

306 Industrial Park Road
Middletown, CT 06457

www.collectorbee.com

Table Of Contents

Introducing The Collector's Value Guide™

Welcome to the Collector's Value Guide™ to Ty® Plush Animals! The Ty® plush line grows bigger and better every year and this guide is filled with the information you need to stay abreast of all the latest happenings. We provide a comprehensive overview of the entire Ty line, starting at the very beginning and taking you all the way through to the newest creations and collections.

Gathered within these pages is the most accurate and up-to-date information on the entire line of Ty collectibles, including the newest additions to the family – *Baby Ty*™ and Beanie *Kids*™. And, of course, we wouldn't leave out old favorites like *Attic Treasures*™, *Beanie Babies*®, *Beanie Buddies*®, *Teenie Beanie Babies*™, *Pillow Pals*® and *Ty Classic*™!

Our Collector's Value Guide™ is a reference guide for collectors of all ages, designed to help you keep track of your collection while providing you with 2000 secondary market values and vital statistics for each piece in the Ty family. Inside this all-new third edition of the Collector's Value Guide™ to Ty® Plush Animals, you'll also find:

★ Descriptions and photos of all the latest releases, including the new *Beanie Babies*

★ A listing of the top five most valuable pieces from the *Attic Treasures*, *Beanie Babies*, *Teenie Beanie Babies*, *Beanie Buddies*, *Pillow Pals* and *Ty Classic* lines

★ An examination of all the different swing tag generations, and their significance in determining secondary market value

★ An overview of the secondary market

★ And much, much more!

The World Of Ty® Plush Animals

It's the dawn of a new millennium, and the Ty Inc. empire is going strong. In less than 20 years, Ty Warner went from quietly producing a small line of plush cats and dogs to being responsible for the biggest toy craze in recent history (*Beanie Babies*, of course). Warner is also a man of great ambition and talent whose success should not come as a surprise to anyone.

Warner made his presence known in the plush industry long before starting his own company. As a sales representative for Dakin, he would arrive to see potential clients in a Rolls Royce, wearing a fur coat and top hat. Even then he knew the value of dramatic presentation.

The History Of Ty Inc.

In the early 1980s, Warner left his job at Dakin to travel overseas. He returned to the United States several years later, and in 1986, he established his own company, which sold a line of plush cats and dogs. The line sold quietly and Ty Inc. was modestly successful. This might have been enough for some, but Warner, known for his attention to detail and commitment to quality, was determined to be the best in the business. This determination would pay off tenfold.

The Ty® Family Tree

Ty Inc. is synonymous, of course, with *Beanie Babies*. But there are many more adorable, cuddly and highly collectible members of the Ty family tree. Currently, there are approximately 1,000 pieces in the Ty family. The *Ty Classic* line has been turning out bears, cats, dogs, hares and every other type of animal under the sun for almost 15 years. And since its introduction in 1993, The Attic Treasures

Collection has been charming collectors everywhere. *Beanie Babies* were born in 1994 and *Pillow Pals* followed in 1995, but Warner did not stop there. In 1997, he surprised collectors by teaming up with McDonald's fast-food restaurants to offer a *Teenie Beanie Babies* promotion. The success of the promotion was unprecedented and was repeated in 1998 and 1999. And for those who still couldn't get enough, in 1998 Ty introduced *Beanie Buddies*, larger-sized mirror images of *Beanie Babies*.

The year 2000 brought even more excitement to the world of Ty collectibles with the introduction of *Baby Ty*, a line of adorable roly-poly animals perfect for babies, and *Beanie Kids*, nine little tykes of varying ethnicities, that, like *Beanie Babies*, have birthdates and poems on their swing tags.

Attic Treasures™

Each collection has its own distinct charm and personality. The *Attic Treasures* line is an assemblage of bears, hares and other characters that are designed in the manner of the old-fashioned, humpbacked bears of days gone by.

The line made its debut with the introduction of 12 bears and rabbits that ranged from 6 to 12 inches tall. These critters came either bare or with a ribbon. In 1995, the name of the collection was changed to "Ty Collectibles," but reverted back to its original name in 1998. A further change occurred with the introduction of the 2000 *Attic Treasures* line. All *Attic Treasures* used to be fully jointed, but many of the new animals aren't, although to a certain extent their limbs are still moveable. One thing that hasn't changed, however, is the nostalgic charm found in each and every *Attic Treasure*.

Beanie Babies®

In 1993, the same year that *Attic Treasures* made its way onto store shelves, another Warner creation was making its first appearance at a Chicago-area trade fair. Nine bean bag critters called *Beanie Babies* made a quiet debut. They hit small gift stores in 1994, but their phenomenon didn't really begin until 1995, when the first three were retired, immediately elevating them to the status of the serious collectible. Suddenly, *Beanie Babies* were the hot item that everyone had to have.

The passion collectors feel for *Beanie Babies* has continued to burn strongly over the years, and at no time was that more evident than when it was announced in a Ty web site newsflash on August 31, 1999 that as of December 31, 1999, all remaining *Beanies* would be retired. Rumors, despair and disbelief flew as collectors tried to determine if this really meant the end for their beloved animals.

Thankfully, it was not to be. A three-day vote to determine the fate of the *Beanie Babies* was conducted via Ty's web site and the telephone, and the victory was decisive – 91% of participants voted for Ty to continue making *Beanie Babies*. And with the recent introduction of 21 new *Beanie Babies*, the future looks very bright indeed for this collection of critters.

Beanie Buddies®

It's been an exciting time for *Beanie Buddies* as well. Since making their debut in 1998, *Beanie Buddies* have grown in popularity – and in size! These characters are made from a special, extremely soft material called "Tylon" and most of them are larger versions of *Beanie Babies*. In early 2000, Ty released 31 new *Beanie Buddies*, including several that have had

a growth spurt! These "large" versions of "Peace," "Hippie" and "Fuzz" – along with "Extra Large Peace," "Extra Large Hippie" and "Jumbo Peace" – added a new dimension to *Beanie Buddies* collecting.

Teenie Beanie Babies™

Speaking of collecting *Beanie Baby* "families," McDonald's *Teenie Beanie Babies* promotions have given collectors the opportunity to do just that. The first promotion took place in April of 1997 and featured 10 tiny replicas of *Beanie Babies* packaged in special bags and distributed in Happy Meals. The promotion was so successful that it was repeated in 1998 and 1999. The 2000 *Teenie Beanie Babies* promotion promises to be no less exciting, as collectors can hardly wait to get their hands on the newest batch of miniature critters.

Pillow Pals®

Proving that Ty's appeal extends to the whole family, in 1995 the company introduced a line of infant-friendly characters called *Pillow Pals*. These guys were made to be kid-proof. From their machine washable bodies to their embroidered eyes and noses (so they could not be torn off by little hands), these pals were just perfect for little ones! In 1999, a change was made to the collection. The once-pastel pals were taken out of production and re-introduced in strong, vibrant colors, following the theory that small children are attracted to bright colors. Yet another change occurred at the end of 1999, when all *Pillow Pals* were retired.

Baby Ty™

It might be that the *Pillow Pals* were retired to make room for the new *Baby Ty* animals. *Baby Ty*, which made its debut in 2000, is a collection of six pastel animals, each with a rattle inside and a red heart embroidered on its body. These soft and cuddly critters are infant friendly as well, and are sure to find their way into many cribs and bassinets this year. Interestingly, the inside of the *Baby Ty* swing tags reads "The Pillow Pals Collection." It's anyone's guess what to make of that, but no matter what they're called, these plush pals are simply irresistible.

Beanie Kids™

Another exciting product also made its debut in early 2000. The *Beanie Kids* are nine tiny tykes, both boys and girls, who come dressed in shorts or dresses. Each "kid" has an adorable belly button and realistic eyes, along with curly or straight hair. With names like "Tumbles," "Boomer," and "Cutie," these kids are sure to add some mischief and fun to the Ty family.

Ty Classic™

With all the excitement over the new lines, it's important not to forget about the forerunner of them all, the *Ty Classic* collection. Known informally among collectors as the *Ty Plush* line, the newly-named *Ty Classic* collection has come a long way since its humble beginnings. From a small litter of cats and dogs, the collection has grown into a menagerie of nearly 400 animals. With a line this large, this menagerie could quickly turn into a zoo. So to make things easier, we've divided the collection into five separate categories: bears, cats, dogs, country and wildlife.

The New Millennium And Beyond

What surprises do Ty Warner and Ty Inc. have in store for us? We can only speculate. But rest assured that the new millennium will bring continued fun, and exciting and varied offerings that collectors all over the globe will enjoy.

What's New For Ty® Plush Animals

This year, Ty introduced two new collections and added new faces to established lines. So let's say "hello" to all of our new friends in Ty land.

Attic Treasures™

AMORE™ . . . This fully jointed bear with a bean-filled belly is the perfect gift for anyone you love "with all your heart."

BERKLEY™ . . . This bear may be a throwback to the 1960s, but his belief that "love is the answer" is timeless.

BEVERLY™ . . . "Beverly's" swirly fur is the perfect complement to the quote on her swing tag – "You Have Me In A Whirlwind."

BLARNEY™ . . . "Blarney" is the ideal gift for those who treasure their Irish heritage (or those who wish they had an Irish heritage!).

BLUSH™ . . . Give this adorable pink bunny to a friend and watch him or her "blush" with pleasure!

CARSON™ ... We think this velvety brown bear is definitely as "sweet as honey," and we're sure that you will, too!

CROMWELL™ ... This bean-filled mouse reminds us that when the cat's away, "the mice will play!"

DARLENE™ ... This fully jointed beige bear's pink outfit is sure to be the height of fashion this season.

FAIRCHILD™ ... If you add "Fairchild" the cat to your collection, he promises to keep an eye on that wily mouse "Cromwell."

HARPER™ ... This cream-colored bear is without a doubt the "cream of the crop!"

HAYES™ ... Let someone special know that you think he or she is "peachy" by giving this adorable peach-colored bear.

ROSALYNE™ ... Wearing a necklace of roses and a rosebud in her hair, this bunny is firm in her belief that "everything is coming up roses."

Baby Ty™

BEARBABY™ ... This loveable, huggable tie-dye bear is a perfect companion for baby.

BUNNYBABY™ ... Like all of the animals in the *Baby Ty* line, this pink and blue bunny is as soft and fluffy as a cloud.

DOGBABY™ ... Children will love "Dogbaby" with its soft colors and floppy ears.

FROGBABY™ ... "Frogbaby's" rattle in his belly makes him just as much fun to shake as he is to hug and squeeze.

LAMYBABY™ ... "Lamybaby's" fur is as soft as can be – perfect for a child to snuggle with.

MONKEYBABY™ ... "Monkeybaby" is sure to be barrels of fun for anyone, old or young.

Beanie Babies®

2000 SIGNATURE BEAR™ ... With its beautiful flocked fur and delicate tulle ribbon, "2000 Signature Bear" is a keepsake for this millennium and beyond!

AURORA™ . . . "Aurora's" beautiful white fur is made of crimped Tylon, making her extra soft and perfect for cuddling on cold nights.

BUSHY™ . . . From his orange foot pads to his "bushy" bright pink and yellow mane, this lion stands out from the crowd with pride.

FLEECIE™ . . . Perfect for spring with her soft yellow fur and pastel lavender ribbon, "Fleecie" would be a wonderful addition to anyone's collection.

FRIGID™ . . . Penguins are a fun-loving bunch, and "Frigid" is no exception! He thinks ice floes are good for sliding and he loves to frolic in the sea.

GLOW™ . . . You'll "glow" with happiness when you add this stunning specimen to your *Beanie Babies* collection.

GRACE™ . . . Like her friend "Hope," this bunny strikes a prayerful pose and reminds us to give thanks for all of our blessings.

HALO II™ . . . The pure white fur of this angel bear provides a stunning contrast to its golden wings and halo. "Halo II" is a natural companion to 1998's "Halo."

MORRIE™ . . . Gliding through the water with ease and grace, this green and yellow eel hopes to find a special place in your collection.

NILES™ . . . Hailing from the Nile region of Egypt, "Niles" the camel crossed many deserts before he joined his *Beanie Baby* friends.

RUFUS™ . . . This adorable pooch tries very hard to talk to his friends; unfortunately, all he can say is, "Ruff!" But it's OK – we love him anyway!

SARGE™ . . . One of two dogs to join the *Beanie* family this year, "Sarge" is a top-notch watch dog who'll protect your Ty plush collection!

SCURRY™ . . . Keep your eyes to the ground, because you won't want to miss this beetle with its beautiful markings scurrying around.

SNEAKY™ . . . This leopard is counting on "Freckles" to show him the ropes in *Beanie Baby* land, but we don't think he'll have any problem "sneaking" in.

SPRINGY™ . . . This lavender bunny is "springing" into the *Beanie Babies* collection just in time for spring and is poised for adventure on the bunny trails of life.

SWAMPY™ . . . Don't be afraid if you see "Swampy" lurking in a river or marsh. He's quite harmless to humans – unless he's hungry!

SWOOP™ . . . This prehistoric pterodactyl "swoops" out of the Jurassic Period and into this year's *Beanie Babies* line.

THE BEGINNING™ . . . This shining star of the new millennium is ready to celebrate the year 2000 (and the return of the *Beanie Babies*) with one and all.

TRUMPET™ . . . This playful elephant is "trumpeting" his happiness for all the world to hear!

WIGGLY™ . . . All eight of this creature's tentacles are "wiggling" with anticipation at the thought of being with his friends "Inky" and "Goochy."

Beanie Buddies®

2000 SIGNATURE BEAR™ . . . One of the few *Beanie Buddies* to precede his *Beanie Baby* counterpart, this bear features a facsimile of Ty Warner's signature on his chest.

BRONTY™ . . . "Bronty" the brontosaurus is delighted that he has finally been made into a *Beanie Buddy* – and so are collectors!

CHOCOLATE . . . Who can resist a serving of "chocolate moose"? We sure can't, and we're pretty sure you won't be able resist this sweet treat, either.

CONGO™ . . . Don't worry, you won't have to go all the way to the Congo to find this gorilla – he's as close as your nearest Ty retailer!

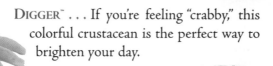

DIGGER™ . . . If you're feeling "crabby," this colorful crustacean is the perfect way to brighten your day.

DOTTY™ . . . With the addition of "Dotty," there are now six dogs available in the *Beanie Buddy* line. Why not collect them all?

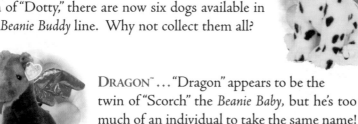

DRAGON™ . . . "Dragon" appears to be the twin of "Scorch" the *Beanie Baby*, but he's too much of an individual to take the same name!

EUCALYPTUS™ . . . Can you guess the favorite snack of this cute koala? Here's a hint – it's the same as his name!

FLIP™ . . . You'll "flip" for this adorable white kitty, one of the latest felines to join the *Beanie Buddy* litter.

FLIPPITY˜ . . . Try as you might, you'll never find a "Flippity" *Beanie Baby* – this adorable bunny is only available in *Beanie Buddy* form!

GOOCHY˜ . . . Don't worry, "Goochy" the jelly-fish doesn't sting. As a matter of fact, you are sure to get along just "swimmingly!"

GROOVY˜ . . . You'll definitely be "feelin' groovy" when you take a trip back to the 1960s with this tie-dyed teddy bear!

HIPPIE˜, LARGE HIPPIE˜ AND EXTRA LARGE HIPPIE˜ . . . Big, bigger and biggest! This tie-dyed trio of bunnies is a "must-have" addition to any collection.

KICKS˜ . . . If you get your "kicks" from soccer or you know an aspiring Mia Hamm, pick up this buddy and make your (or someone else's) day!

LARGE FUZZ˜ . . . Yet another addition to the "plus-sized" family of *Beanie Buddies*, "Large Fuzz" is sure to delight collectors.

LARGE PEACE˜, EXTRA LARGE PEACE˜ AND JUMBO PEACE˜ . . . Spread some "peace" and love with this tie-dyed troupe of varying sizes.

LIPS˜ . . . Pucker up! This brightly colored tropical fish with big red lips wants to give you a giant fish kiss.

LIZZY˜ . . . "Lizzy" the tie-dyed *Beanie Baby* was only produced for six months. Let's hope that this many-colored "Lizzy" sticks around longer.

LUCKY˜ . . . You'll be very "lucky" indeed if this lovely ladybug crosses your path.

NANOOK˜ . . . "Nanook" the husky is the perfect buddy to cuddle up with on long, cold winter nights.

OSITO˜ . . . Continuing in the tradition of the internationally themed *Beanie Buddies*, "Osito" the bear sports the Mexican flag on its chest.

RAINBOW˜. . . With all the colors on this tie-dyed chameleon, "Rainbow" should be able to blend into any environment with ease.

SPEEDY˜ . . . "Speedy" may not be first at the finish line, but he will certainly race his way into your heart.

TY 2K™ ... New Year's Eve has come and gone, and so has this confetti-dappled bear who partied his way into the new millennium.

VALENTINO™ ... "Valentino" loves being a *Beanie Buddy*. He just wishes that the folks at Ty would hurry up and make his sweetheart "Valentina" a *Buddy*, too!

WEENIE™ ... "Weenie" will wiggle with delight if you take him home with you! He can't wait to play with the other dogs in your collection.

ZIP™ ... With a red ribbon around his neck, "Zip" is waiting to be given to someone special.

Beanie Kids™

ANGEL™, CURLY™, CUTIE™, GINGER™ AND PRECIOUS™ ... These adorable *Beanie Kids* girls spread happiness with their sweet smiles and huggable bodies.

BOOMER™, CHIPPER™, RASCAL™ AND TUMBLES™ ... These mischievous *Beanie Kids* boys are determined to charm their way into your arms and your collection.

Ty Classic™

BAMBOO™ ... If you've never met a bear you didn't like, this picturesque panda will be a welcome addition to your collection.

BELVEDERE™ ... From his lustrous mixed grey and gold fur to his delicate organza ribbon, "Belvedere" is a bear with class to spare!

BRODERICK™ ... Even though "Broderick" may look a little "blue" under his brown coat, he won't be if you'll take him home with you!

DASH™ ... Grrr! "Dash" likes to think he's a ferocious tiger, but we all know he's just a pussycat who'd love to prowl his way into your heart.

DOT™ ... "Dot" the leopard proudly stands poised to show off her beautiful spots.

DUSTER™ ... No, that's not a mop – it's a dog! "Duster" is a Lhasa apso that's so lifelike he's the next best thing to having a real dog!

JAKE™ ... "Jake" is a popular name in *Ty Classic* land, but this "Jake" is a tad different than his monkey namesakes – he's a gorilla!

LILACBEARY™ ... Can you guess what this bear's favorite flower is? "Lilacbeary" is a soft, cuddly and colorful addition to any bearlover's collection.

MYSTERY™ . . . It's a "mystery" to us why anyone wouldn't love this "purrfectly" beautiful cat!

PETER™ . . . "Peter" is a wonderfully soft bunny who's looking for the "bunny trail" that will lead him to you!

PRISSY™ . . . She may be a little bit "prissy," but that doesn't mean that this fluffy feline wouldn't make a wonderful addition to any litter of kitties!

SCOOTER™ . . . "Scooter" is an adorable understuffed brown dog who's always ready to play, night or day.

SERENGETI™ . . . If you went on an African safari, perhaps you'd see a zebra that looks just like the appropriately named (and maned) "Serengeti."

SHADOW™ . . . "Shadow" is certainly sitting pretty in her position as one of the newest cats on the *Ty Classic* block.

SMOKEY™ . . . This fluffy Persian can be posed in just about any position, but the one she likes best is cuddled up next to you!

STRETCH™ ... Aaaahhhh! We can all use a good "stretch" every now and then, and no one knows that better than cats, as "Stretch" proves.

TAFFYBEARY™ ... "Taffybeary" is caramel-colored with a tint of pink! And with a name like "Taffybeary," he's sure to add some sweetness to any collection.

TOFFEE™ ... This terrier is no terror. He's just a cute and friendly pup who can't wait to play with you!

YESTERBEAR™ ... The "Yesterbear" triplets, with their luxurious fur and bean-filled paws, are both classic and cuddly.

Introducing . . .
"Sakura™" the Beanie Baby®!

"Sakura," Ty's first Japanese exclusive, joined the *Beanie Baby* family on March 17, 2000. Her lovely name translates to "cherry blossom," which is Japan's national flower.

Recent Retirements

The biggest retirement news of 1999, was, of course, the announcement that on December 23, all remaining *Beanie Babies* would retire. But five *Attic Treasures*, 28 *Beanie Buddies*, 16 *Pillow Pals* and six *Ty Classic* critters also retired between October 1999 and March 2000. Following is a list of these pieces.

ATTIC TREASURES™

Allura™, Amore™, Beezee™, Spruce™, Tyra™

BEANIE BABIES®

1999 Holiday Teddy™, 1999 Signature Bear™, Almond™, Amber™, B.B. Bear™, Beak™, Butch™, Cheeks™, Chipper™, Clubby II™, Early™, Eucalyptus™, Flitter™, Fuzz™, Germania™, GiGi™, Goatee™, Goochy™, Groovy™, Halo™, Honks™, Hope™, Jabber™, Jake™, Kicks™, Knuckles™, KuKu™, Lips™, Luke™, Mac™, Maple™, Millennium™, Mooch™, Neon™, Osito™, Paul™, Pecan™, Prickles™, Roam™, Rocket™, Sammy™, Scaly™,

Scat™, Schweetheart™, Scorch™, Sheets™, Silver™, Slippery™, Slowpoke™, Spangle™, Swirly™, The End™, Tiny™, Tiptoe™, Tracker™, Ty 2K™, Valentina™, Wallace™, Whisper™

BEANIE BUDDIES®

Bongo™, Bubbles™, Chilly™, Chip™, Erin™, Fetch™, Gobbles™, Hippity™, Hope™, Humphrey™, Inch™, Jabber™, Jake™, Millennium™, Peanut™, Peking™, Pinky™, Pumkin'™, Rover™, Schweetheart™, Smoochy™, Snort™, Snowboy™, Spinner™, Squealer™, Stretch™, Teddy™, Tracker™, Ty 2K™, Waddle™

PILLOW PALS®

Antlers™, Ba Ba™, Carrots™, Chewy™, Huggy™, Kolala™, Meow™, Paddles™, Ribbit™, Rusty™, Sherbet™, Snap™, Sparkler™, Squirt™, Swinger™, Woof™

TY CLASSIC™

Bows™, Buttons™, Churchill™, Crystal™, Faith™, George™

These are the five most valuable *Attic Treasures*, as determined by their secondary market values. Only "Tyra" is a later-generation character. All of the rest are from the first generation, and some of them are variations of the original piece.

1

WOOLIE™ (#6011)
Issued 1993 - Retired 1993
Secondary Market Value: ❶- $1,000

2

TYRA™ (#6201)
Issued 1999 - Retired 1999
Secondary Market Value: ❼- $975

3

HENRY™ (#6005)
Blue Ribbon/Gold Version
Issued 1993 - Retired 1997
Secondary Market Value: ❶- $900

4

REGGIE™ (#6004)
Issued 1993 - Retired 1995
Red Ribbon Version
Secondary Market Value: ❶- $515
Navy Ribbon Version
Secondary Market Value: ❶- $400

5

GILBERT™ (#6015)
Issued 1993 - Retired 1993
Secondary Market Value: ❶- $390

Beanie Babies® Top Five

There are the five most valuable *Beanie Babies*, as determined by their secondary market values. Three of them were never made available to the general public, making them very valuable on the secondary market.

#1 BEAR™ (N/A)
Exclusive Ty Sales Representative Gift
Issued December 11-14, 1998
Secondary Market Value:
Special Tag – $9,200

BILLIONAIRE 2™ (N/A)
Exclusive Ty Employee Gift
Issued September 1999
Secondary Market Value:
Special Tag – $5,800

PEANUT™ (#4062)
Dark Blue Version
Issued 1995 - Retired 1998
Secondary Market Value:
– $4,400

TEDDY™ (VIOLET, #4055)
New Face/Employee Bear w/Red Tush Tag
Issued 1994 - Retired 1996
Secondary Market Value:
No Swing Tag – $3,800

NANA™ (#4067)
Issued 1995 - Retired 1995
Secondary Market Value:
– $3,700

Beanie Buddies® Top Five

These are the five most valuable *Beanie Buddies*, as determined by their secondary market values for first generation tags. This is the first year that secondary market values have been assigned to the *Buddies*, as previously, few of them had been retired.

QUACKERS™ (#9302)
Without Wings
Issued 1998 - Retired 1999
Secondary Market Value: – $250

TWIGS™ (#9308)
Issued 1998 - Retired 1999
Secondary Market Value: – $215

BRITANNIA™ (#9601)
Exclusive to the United Kingdom
Issued 1999 – Current
Secondary Market Value: – $150

MAPLE™ (#9600)
Exclusive to Canada
Issued 1999 - Current
Secondary Market Value: – $135

PEANUT™ (#9300)
Light Blue Version
Issued 1998 - Retired 2000
Secondary Market Value: – $50

Teenie Beanie Babies™ Top Five

These are the five most valuable *Teenie Beanie Babies*, as determined by their secondary market values. The *Teenie Beanie Babies* released in the earlier part of the first promotion generally have a greater secondary market value than other pieces, although all *Teenie Beanie Babies* have a secondary market value.

PINKY™
1st Promotion, #2
Issued 1997 - Retired 1997
Secondary Market Value: $36

PATTI™
1st Promotion, #1
Issued 1997 - Retired 1997
Secondary Market Value: $30

CHOPS™
1st Promotion, #3
Issued 1997 - Retired 1997
Secondary Market Value: $28

CHOCOLATE™
1st Promotion, #4
Issued 1997 - Retired 1997
Secondary Market Value: $24

SEAMORE™
1st Promotion, #7
Issued 1997 - Retired 1997
Secondary Market Value: $24

Pillow Pals® Top Five

These are the five most valuable *Pillow Pals*, as determined by their secondary market values. All of the *Pillow Pals* were retired in 1999. The ones found on this list are critters that were retired several years ago.

RIBBIT™ (#3006)
Issued 1995 - Retired 1996
Secondary Market Value: $410

SNAP™ (#3007)
Issued 1995 - Retired 1996
Secondary Market Value: $365

MEOW™ (#3011)
Gray Version
Issued 1997 - Retired 1998
Secondary Market Value: $140

SNUGGY™ (#3001)
Issued 1995 - Retired 1998
Secondary Market Value: $28

HUGGY™ (#3002)
Issued 1995 - Retired 1998
Secondary Market Value: $27

COLLECTOR'S
VALUE GUIDE™

Ty Classic™ Top Five

These are the five most valuable *Ty Classics*, as determined by their secondary market values. The *Ty Classic* top five includes four animals – a dog and three cats – that were all produced in 1986, the year the line made its debut.

SUPER SCHNAPPS™ (#3002)
Issued 1986 - Retired 1986
Secondary Market Value: $1,400

BABY KIMCHI™ (#2004)
Issued 1986 - Retired 1986
Secondary Market Value: $1,350

BABY BUTTERBALL™ (#2006)
Issued 1986 - Retired 1986
Secondary Market Value: $1,300

BABY OSCAR™ (#2008)
Issued 1986 - Retired 1986
Secondary Market Value: $1,275

1991 TY COLLECTABLE BEAR™ (#5500)
Issued 1991 - Retired 1991
Secondary Market Value: $1,250

How To Use Your Value Guide

① Locate your piece in the Value Guide. The guide lists *Attic Treasures* first, followed by *Baby Ty, Beanie Babies, Beanie Buddies, Teenie Beanie Babies, Beanie Kids, Pillow Pals* and *Ty Classic*. The *Ty Classic* sec-

Abby™
8" • Bear • #6027
Issued: 1995 • Retired: 1998
A. Overalls w/Flower (1998)
B. Overalls (1996-97)
C. Ribbon (1995-96)
Market Value: ❷–$23 ❸–$25
❹–$70 ❺–$70 ❻–$122

tion is categorized by bears, cats, dogs, country and wildlife. All pieces are listed alphabetically within each collection. To find a piece more quickly, turn to the Animal Index on page 236 or the Alphabetical Index on page 247. Note: Some items included are prototypes and may differ slightly from the actual piece. All sizes are approximate and may vary.

② Find the secondary market value of your piece. Some values are listed as "N/E," meaning the secondary market value for that piece has not been established. *Attic Treasures, Beanie Babies* and *Beanie Buddies* secondary market values are determined by the generation tag attached to the piece (for more details, see page 224). The market values for these pieces are listed next to the appropriate generation tag symbols. Variations with secondary market values are listed by corresponding letter or description next to their market values. For each current piece, write in the current

Attic Treasures™

Date Purchased	Tag Gen.	Price Paid	Value
1. 3/98	3	?	$70
2.			
3.			

Totals

market price on the space provided (**⑦**– $_____), which is usually the price you paid. All values listed are for pieces in mint condition.

③ Record the original price (what you actually paid), as well as the current value of the piece. Mark the prices in the corresponding boxes at the bottom of the page. Be sure to use a pencil so you can change the totals as your collection grows!

④ Calculate the total value for the entire page by adding together all of the boxes in each column.

⑤ Transfer the totals from each page to the Total Value Of My Collection worksheets on pages 212-214.

⑥ Add all of the totals together to determine the overall value of your collection.

Attic Treasures™

Twelve new critters joined the collection in January 2000, bringing the total number of members in the *Attic Treasures* family to 147 (the "Curly" family, once part of the group, have moved to *Ty Classics*). Swing tags did not change this year, but it is important to note that *Attic Treasures* are valued according to their swing tag generation.

ATTIC TREASURES™ TAG KEY	
⑦– 7th Generation	③– 3rd Generation
⑥– 6th Generation	②– 2nd Generation
⑤– 5th Generation	①– 1st Generation
④– 4th Generation	

1

Abby™
8" • Bear • #6027
Issued: 1995 • Retired: 1998
A. Overalls w/Flower (1998)
B. Overalls (1996-97)
C. Ribbon (1995-96)
Market Value: ⑥–$23 ⑤–$25
④–$70 ③–$70 ②–$122

2

Allura™
8" • Bear • #6058
Issued: 1999 • Current
Market Value: ⑦–$_____

3

Amethyst™
13" • Cat • #6131
Issued: 1998 • Retired: 1998
Market Value: ⑥–$25

Attic Treasures™

	Date Purchased	Tag Gen.	Price Paid	Value
1.				
2.				
3.				

Totals

4 New!

Amore™
8" • Bear • #6206
Issued: 2000 • Current
Market Value: ❼–$_____

5

Azalea™
8" • Bunny • #6093
Issued: 1999 • Current
Market Value: ❼–$_____

6

Azure™
8" • Bear • #6055
Issued: 1999 • Current
Market Value: ❼–$_____

7

Baby Curly™
(moved to Ty Classic™ in 2000)
12" • Bear • #5018 • Issued: 1993 • Current
A. Leaf Sweater, Ty Classic Swing Tag (2000-Current)
B. USA Sweater, Attic Treasures Swing Tag (1999-2000)
C. USA Sweater, Ty Plush Swing Tag (1998-1999)
D. Ribbon, Ty Plush Swing Tag (1993-98)
Market Value: A–$_____ B–**$40** C–**$30** D–**$20**

Attic Treasures™

	Date Purchased	Tag Gen.	Price Paid	Value
4.				
5.				
6.				
7.				
8.				

Totals

8

Barry™
8" • Bear • #6073
Issued: 1997 • Retired: 1997
Market Value: ❺–**$102**

9

Beargundy™
8" • Bear • #6205
Issued: 1999 • Current
Market Value: 7–$_____

10

Bearington™
14" • Bear • #6102
Issued: 1998 • Retired: 1998
Market Value: 6–$24

11

Bearkhardt™
8" • Bear • #6204
Issued: 1999 • Current
Market Value: 7–$_____

12

Beezee™
8" • Bumble Bee • #6088
Issued: 1999 • Retired: 1999
Market Value: 7–$13

13

Benjamin™
9" • Rabbit • #6023
Issued: 1995 • Retired: 1997
A. Sweater (1996-97)
B. Ribbon (1995-96)
Market Value: 5–$55 2–$105

Attic Treasures™

	Date Purchased	Tag Gen.	Price Paid	Value
9.				
10.				
11.				
12.				
13.				

Totals

35

14

New!

Berkley™
8" • Bear • #6218
Issued: 2000 • Current
Market Value: ⑦–$_____

15

New!

Beverly™
8" • Bear • #6210
Issued: 2000 • Current
Market Value: ⑦–$_____

16

New!

Blarney™
8" • Bear • #6215
Issued: 2000 • Current
Market Value: ⑦–$_____

17

Bloom™
16" • Rabbit • #6122
Issued: 1998 • Retired: 1998
Market Value: ⑥–$26

Attic Treasures™

	Date Purchased	Tag Gen.	Price Paid	Value
14.				
15.				
16.				
17.				
18.				

Totals

18

Bluebeary™
8" • Bear • #6080
Issued: 1998 • Retired: 1999
Market Value: ⑦–$12 ⑥–$17

19 New! ✓

Blush™
8" • Bunny • #6208
Issued: 2000 • Current
Market Value: ❼–$_____

20 ✓

Bonnie™
9" • Chick • #6075
Issued: 1998 • Current
Market Value: ❼–$_____ ❻–$14

21

Boris™
12" • Bear • #6041
Issued: 1996 • Retired: 1997
A. Vest (1996-97)
B. No Clothes (1996)
Market Value: ❺–$50

22 ✓

Breezy™
8" • Bear • #6057
Issued: 1999 • Current
Market Value: ❼–$_____

23

Brewster™
9" • Dog • #6034
Issued: 1995 • Retired: 1997
A. Overalls (1996-97)
B. No Clothes (1995-96)
Market Value: ❺–$32 ❹–$48
❸–$58 ❷–$70

Attic Treasures™

	Date Purchased	Tag Gen.	Price Paid	Value
19.				
20.				
21.				
22.				
23.				

Totals

24

Brisbane™
8" • Koala • #6052
Issued: 1999 • Current
Market Value: ❼–$_____

25

Bugsy™
8" • Ladybug • #6089
Issued: 1999 • Retired: 1999
Market Value: ❼–$13

26

Camelia™
8" • Bunny • #6094
Issued: 1999 • Retired: 1999
Market Value: ❼–$12

27

Carlton™
16" • Bear • #6064
Issued: 1996 • Retired: 1997
A. Overalls (1996-97)
B. Ribbon (1996)
**Market Value: ❺–$47 (Overalls),
$72 (Ribbon)**

28

New!

Carson™
8" • Bear • #6216
Issued: 2000 • Current
Market Value: ❼–$_____

Attic Treasures™

	Date Purchased	Tag Gen.	Price Paid	Value
24.				
25.				
26.				
27.				
28.				

Totals

29

Casanova™
8" • Bear • #6073
Issued: 1998 • Retired: 1999
Market Value: **7**–$12 **6**–$15

30

Cassie™
12" • Bear • #6028
Issued: 1995 • Retired: 1997
A. Bloomers (1996-97)
B. Ribbon (1995-96)
Market Value: **5**–$75 **4**–$100
3–$140 **2**–$185

31

Cawley™
10" • Crow • #6090
Issued: 1999 • Current
Market Value: **7**–$_____

32

Charles™
12" • Bear • #6039
Issued: 1996 • Retired: 1997
A. Overalls (1996-97)
B. No Clothes (1996)
Market Value: **5**–$46

33

Checkers™
8" • Panda • #6031
Issued: 1995 • Current
A. No Clothes (1998-Current)
B. Vest (1996-97)
C. No Clothes (1995-96)
Market Value: **7**–$_____ **6**–$15
5–$23 **4**–$80 **3**–$97 **2**–$115

Attic Treasures™

	Date Purchased	Tag Gen.	Price Paid	Value
29.				
30.				
31.				
32.				
33.				

Totals

34

Chelsea™
8" • Bear • #6070
Issued: 1996 • Retired: 1998
Market Value: *6*–$18 *5*–$20

35

Cheri™
8" • Poodle • #6200
Issued: 1999 • Current
Market Value: *7*–$_____

36

Christopher™
8" • Bear • #6071
Issued: 1996 • Retired: 1998
Market Value: *6*–$19 *5*–$22

37

Clifford™
12" • Bear • #6003
Issued: 1993 • Retired: 1995
A. Green Ribbon (1994-95)
B. Red Ribbon (1993)
Market Value: *1*–$300 (Red Ribbon),
$260 (Green Ribbon)

38

Clyde™
12" • Bear • #6040
Issued: 1996 • Retired: 1997
A. Vest (1996-97)
B. No Clothes (1996)
Market Value: *5*–$48

Attic Treasures™

	Date Purchased	Tag Gen.	Price Paid	Value
34.				
35.				
36.				
37.				
38.				

Totals

39

Cody™
8" • Bear • #6030
Issued: 1995 • Current
Market Value: **7**–$_____ **6**–$15
5–$17 **4**–$46 **3**–$70 **2**–$95

40

Colby™
11" • Mouse • #6043
Issued: 1996 • Retired: 1997
A. Bloomers (1996-97)
B. No Clothes (1996)
Market Value: **5**–$55

41

Copperfield™
16" • Bear • #6060
Issued: 1996 • Retired: 1997
A. Sweater (1996-97)
B. Ribbon (1996)
Market Value: **5**–$65 (Sweater),
$140 (Ribbon)

42 New!

Cromwell™
8" • Mouse • #6221
Issued: 2000 • Current
Market Value: **7**–$_____

Attic Treasures™

	Date Purchased	Tag Gen.	Price Paid	Value
39.				
40.				
41.				
42.				

Totals

43

Curly™
(moved to Ty Classic™ in 2000)

18" • Bear • #5302 • Issued: 1991 • Current
A. 18", Umbrella Sweater, Ty Classic Swing Tag (2000-Current)
B. 18", Flag Sweater, Attic Treasures Swing Tag (1999-2000)
C. 18", Flag Sweater, Ty Plush Swing Tag (1998-1999)
D. 18", Ribbon, Ty Plush Swing Tag (1993-98)
E. 22", Ty Plush Swing Tag (1991-92)
Market Value: A–$_____ B–$30 C–$30 D–$25 E–$25

44

Curly Bunny™
(moved to Ty Classic™ in 2000)

22" • Bunny • #8017 • Issued: 1992 • Current
A. Sweater, Ty Classic Swing Tag (2000-Current)
B. Sweater, Attic Treasures Swing Tag (1999-2000)
C. Sweater, Ty Plush Swing Tag (1998-1999)
D. No Clothes, Ty Plush Swing Tag (1992-98)
Market Value: A–$_____ B–$45 C–$25 D–$20

45

Curly Bunny™
(moved to Ty Classic™ in 2000)

22" • Bunny • #8017 • Issued: 1992 • Current
A. Sweater, Ty Classic Swing Tag (2000-Current)
B. Sweater, Attic Treasures Swing Tag (1999-2000)
C. Sweater, Ty Plush Swing Tag (1998-1999)
D. No Clothes, Ty Plush Swing Tag (1992-98)
Market Value: A–$_____ B–$45 C–$25 D–$20

46

New!

Darlene™
8" • Bear • #6213
Issued: 2000 • Current
Market Value: ❼–$_____

Attic Treasures™

	Date Purchased	Tag Gen.	Price Paid	Value
43.				
44.				
45.				
46.				
47.				

Totals

47

Dexter™
9" • Bear • #6009
Issued: 1993 • Retired: 1997
A. Overalls (1996-97)
B. Ribbon (1993-96)
**Market Value: ❺–$27 ❹–$60
❸–$65 ❷–$95 ❶–$110**

48

Dickens™
8" • Bear • #6038
Issued: 1996 • Retired: 1998
A. No Clothes (1998)
B. Overalls (1996-97)
C. No Clothes (1996)
Market Value: ⑥–$20 ⑤–$22 ④–$53

49

Digby™
12" • Bear • #6013
Issued: 1994 • Retired: 1997
A. Vest (1996-97)
B. Ribbon (1994-96)
Market Value: ⑤–$65 ④–$90
③–N/E ②–N/E ①–$285

50

Domino™
12" • Panda • #6042
Issued: 1996 • Retired: 1997
A. Overalls (1996-97)
B. No Clothes (1996)
Market Value: ⑤–$40

51

Ebony™
15" • Cat • #6063
Issued: 1996 • Retired: 1997
A. Bloomers (1996-97)
B. Ribbon (1996)
Market Value: ⑤–$40 (Bloomers),
$190 (Ribbon)

52

Ebony™
13" • Cat • #6130
Issued: 1998 • Retired: 1998
Market Value: ⑥–$23

Attic Treasures™

	Date Purchased	Tag Gen.	Price Paid	Value
48.				
49.				
50.				
51.				
52.				

Totals

Attic Treasures™

53

Emily™
12" • Bear • #6016
Issued: 1994 • Retired: 1997
A. Dress/Hat (1996-97)
B. Bow (1995-96)
C. Ribbon/Small Feet (1994-95)
D. Ribbon/Big Feet (1994)
Market Value: ⑤–$90 ④–$100
③–$135 ②–$130 ①–$165 (Bow), $160
(Ribbon/Small Feet), $210 (Ribbon/Big Feet)

54

Esmerelda™
8" • Bear • #6086
Issued: 1998 • Retired: 1998
Market Value: ⑦–$20 ⑥–$24

55

Eve™
12" • Bear • #6106
Issued: 1998 • Current
Market Value: ⑦–$_____ ⑥–$16

56

Fairbanks™
8" • Bear • #6059
Issued: 1999 • Current
Market Value: ⑦–$_____

Attic Treasures™

	Date Purchased	Tag Gen.	Price Paid	Value
53.				
54.				
55.				
56.				
57.				

Totals

57

New!

Fairchild™
8" • Cat • #6220
Issued: 2000 • Current
Market Value: ⑦–$_____

58

Fraser™
8" • Bear • #6010
Issued: 1993 • Retired: 1998
A. Sweater (1996-98)
B. Ribbon (1993-96)
Market Value: **6**–$20 **5**–$32 **4**–$65
3–$68 **2**–$115 **1**–$175

59

Frederick™
8" • Bear • #6072
Issued: 1996 • Retired: 1997
Market Value: **5**–$50

60

Gem™
13" • Bear • #6107
Issued: 1998 • Retired: 1998
Market Value: **7**–$18

61 ✓

Georgette™
9" • Goose • #6091
Issued: 1999 • Current
Market Value: **7**–$_____

62 ✓

Georgia™
8" • Bunny • #6095
Issued: 1999 • Current
Market Value: **7**–$_____

Attic Treasures™

	Date Purchased	Tag Gen.	Price Paid	Value
58.				
59.				
60.				
61.				
62.				

Totals

63

Gilbert™
8" • Bear • #6006
Issued: 1993 • Retired: 1997
A. Overalls (1996-97)
B. Ribbon (1993-96)
Market Value: –$33 ①–$200

64

Gilbert™
8" • Bear • #6015
Issued: 1993 • Retired: 1993
Market Value: ①–$390

65

Gloria™
12" • Rabbit • #6123
Issued: 1998 • Retired: 1998
Market Value: ⑥–$50

66

Gordon™
13" • Bear • #6110
Issued: 1999 • Retired: 1999
Market Value: ⑦–$20

67

Grace™
12" • Hippopotamus • #6142
Issued: 1998 • Retired: 1998
Market Value: ⑥–$22

Attic Treasures™

	Date Purchased	Tag Gen.	Price Paid	Value
63.				
64.				
65.				
66.				
67.				

Totals

68

Grady™
16" • Bear • #6051
Issued: 1996 • Retired: 1997
A. Vest (1996-97)
B. Ribbon (1996)
Market Value: ⑤–$75

69

Grant™
13" • Bear • #6101
Issued: 1998 • Retired: 1999
Market Value: ⑦–$17 ⑥–$22

70

Grover™
16" • Bear • #6050
Issued: 1995 • Retired: 1997
A. Overalls (1996-97)
B. Ribbon (1995-96)
Market Value: ⑤–$35 ④–$65
③–$80 ②–$95

71

Grover™
13" • Bear • #6100
Issued: 1998 • Retired: 1998
Market Value: ⑥–$27

72

Grover Gold™
16" • Bear • #6051
Issued: 1995 • Retired: 1997
A. Vest (Est. 1997)
B. Ribbon (Est. 1995)
Market Value: ⑤–$50 ④–$65

Attic Treasures™

	Date Purchased	Tag Gen.	Price Paid	Value
68.				
69.				
70.				
71.				
72.				

Totals

Attic Treasures™

73

Gwyndolyn™
8" • Bear • #6209
Issued: 1999 • Current
Market Value: ❼–$_____

74

New!

Harper™
8" • Bear • #6214
Issued: 2000 • Current
Market Value: ❼–$_____

75

New!

Hayes™
8" • Bear • #6212
Issued: 2000 • Current
Market Value: ❼–$_____

76

Heartley™
12" • Bear • #6111
Issued: 1999 • Current
Market Value: ❼–$_____

77

Heather™
20" • Rabbit • #6061
Issued: 1996 • Retired: 1997
A. Overalls (1996-97)
B. Ribbon (1996)
Market Value: ❺–$55 (Overalls),
$90 (Ribbon)

Attic Treasures™

	Date Purchased	Tag Gen.	Price Paid	Value
73.				
74.				
75.				
76.				
77.				

Totals

78

Henry™
8" • Bear • #6005
Issued: 1993 • Retired: 1997
A. Overalls (1996-97)
B. Green Ribbon/Brown (1994-96)
C. Blue Ribbon/Gold (1993)
D. Red Ribbon/Gold (1993)
Market Value: ⑤–**$35**
–**$190 (Green Ribbon/Brown),
$900 (Blue Ribbon/Gold),
N/E (Red Ribbon/Gold)**

79

NT

Iris™
10" • Rabbit • #6077
Issued: 1998 • Retired: 1998
Market Value: ⑦–**$15** ⑥–**$16**

80

Isabella™
13" • Bear • #6109
Issued: 1998 • Current
Market Value: ⑦–**$_____**

81

Ivan™
8" • Bear • #6029
Issued: 1995 • Retired: 1999
Market Value: ⑦–**$12** ⑥–**$17**
⑤–**$26** ④–**$67** ③–**$78** ②–**$110**

82

Ivory™
15" • Cat • #6062
Issued: 1996 • Retired: 1997
A. Overalls (1996-97)
B. Ribbon (1996)
Market Value: ⑤–**$55 (Overalls),
$120 (Ribbon)**

Attic Treasures™

	Date Purchased	Tag Gen.	Price Paid	Value
78.				
79.				
80.				
81.				
82.				

Attic Treasures™

83

Ivy™
10" • Rabbit • #6076
Issued: 1998 • Retired: 1998
Market Value: ❼–$17 ❻–$17

84

Jack™
(exclusive to the United Kingdom)
13" • Bear • #6989
Issued: 1998 • Current
Market Value: ❼–$_____ ❻–$58

85

Jangle™
8" • Bear • #6082
Issued: 1998 • Retired: 1998
Market Value: ❼–$23

86

Jeremy™
12" • Hare • #6008
Issued: 1993 • Retired: 1997
A. Overalls (1997)
B. Vest (1996-97)
C. Ribbon (1993-96)
Market Value: ❺–$44 ❹–$79
❸–$85 ❷–$150 ❶–$185

Attic Treasures™

	Date Purchased	Tag Gen.	Price Paid	Value
83.				
84.				
85.				
86.				
87.				

Totals

87

Justin™
14" • Monkey • #6044
Issued: 1996 • Retired: 1997
A. Sweater (1996-97)
B. No Clothes (1996)
Market Value: ❺–$60

88

Katrina™
8" • Cat • #6054
Issued: 1999 • Current
Market Value: ❼–$____

89

King™
9" • Frog • #6049
Issued: 1996 • Retired: 1997
A. Cape (1996-97)
B. No Clothes (1996)
Market Value: ❺–$45

90

King™
11" • Frog • #6140
Issued: 1998 • Retired: 1998
Market Value: ❻–$30

91

Large Curly™
(moved to Ty Classic™ in 2000)
26" • Bear • #9019 • Issued: 1992 • Current
A. Flower Sweater, Ty Classic Swing Tag (2000-Current)
B. Flag Sweater, Attic Treasures Swing Tag (1999-2000)
C. Flag Sweater, Ty Plush Swing Tag (1998-1999)
D. Ribbon, Ty Plush Swing Tag (1992-98)
Market Value: A–$____ B–$55 C–$40 D–$30

92

Laurel™
8" • Bear • #6081
Issued: 1998 • Retired: 1998
Market Value: ❼–$25

Attic Treasures™

	Date Purchased	Tag Gen.	Price Paid	Value
88.				
89.				
90.				
91.				
92.				

Totals

Attic Treasures™

93

Lawrence™
9" • Camel • #6053
Issued: 1999 • Current
Market Value: ❼–$_____

94

Lilly™
9" • Lamb • #6037
Issued: 1995 • Retired: 1998
A. Bloomers (1996-98)
B. Ribbon (1995-96)
Market Value: ❻–$23 ❺–$30
❹–$100 ❸–$110 ❷–$140

95

Mackenzie™
(exclusive to Canada)
13" • Bear • #6999
Issued: 1998 • Current
Market Value: ❼–$_____ ❻–$72

96

Madison™
10" • Cow • #6035
Issued: 1995 • Retired: 1998
A. Overalls (1996-98)
B. Ribbon (1995-96)
Market Value: ❻–$25 ❺–$32
❹–$76 ❸–$95 ❷–$125

Attic Treasures™

	Date Purchased	Tag Gen.	Price Paid	Value
93.				
94.				
95.				
96.				
97.				

97

Malcolm™
12" • Bear • #6026
Issued: 1995 • Retired: 1997
A. Sweater (1996-97)
B. Ribbon (1995-96)
Market Value: ❺–$45 ❹–$76
❸–$90 ❷–$140

Value Guide — Ty® Plush Animals

98

Malcolm™
13" • Bear • #6112
Issued: 1999 • Current
Market Value: ⑦-$_____

99

Mason™
8" • Bear • #6020
Issued: 1995 • Retired: 1998
A. Sweater (1996-98)
B. Ribbon (1995-96)
Market Value: ⑥-$24 ⑤-$28
④-$45 ③-$90 ②-$145

100

Montgomery™
15" • Moose • #6143
Issued: 1998 • Retired: 1998
Market Value: ⑥-$24

101

Morgan™
8" • Monkey • #6018
Issued: 1994 • Retired: 1998
A. Vest (1996-98)
B. No Clothes/Shaved Face (1996)
C. Ribbon/Furry Face (1994-95)
Market Value: ⑥-$20 ⑤-$28
②-N/E ①-$150

102

Murphy™
9" • Dog • #6033
Issued: 1995 • Retired: 1997
A. Overalls (1996-97)
B. No Clothes (1995-96)
Market Value: ⑤-$33 ④-$50
③-$72 ②-$80

Attic Treasures™

	Date Purchased	Tag Gen.	Price Paid	Value
98.				
99.				
100.				
101.				
102.				

Totals

Attic Treasures™

53

Attic Treasures™

103

Nicholas™
8" • Bear • #6015
Issued: 1994 • Retired: 1998
A. Sweater (1996-98)
B. Ribbon (1994-96)
Market Value: ❻–$20 ❺–$24
❹–$200 ❸–N/E ❷–N/E ❶–$300

104

Nola™
12" • Bear • #6014
Issued: 1994 • Retired: 1997
A. Dress/Hat (1996-97)
B. Bow/Small Feet (1995-96)
C. Ribbon/Big Feet (1994-95)
Market Value: ❺–$85 ❹–$100
❸–$130 ❷–$170 ❶–$200 (Bow/Small Feet), $250 (Ribbon/Big Feet)

105

✓

Orion™
8" • Bear • #6207
Issued: 1999 • Current
Market Value: ❼–$_____

106

N/T

Oscar™
8" • Bear • #6025
Issued: 1995 • Retired: 1998
A. Overalls (1996-98)
B. Ribbon (1995-96)
Market Value: ❻–$24 ❺–$35
❹–$60 ❸–$75 ❷–$105

Attic Treasures™

	Date Purchased	Tag Gen.	Price Paid	Value
103.				
104.				
105.				
106.				
107.				

Totals

107

✓

Penelope™
9" • Pig • #6036
Issued: 1995 • Retired: 1997
A. Overalls (1996-97)
B. No Clothes (1995-96)
Market Value: ❺–$50 ❹–$80
❸–$100 ❷–$120

Attic Treasures™

108 ✓

Peppermint™
8" • Polar Bear • #6074
Issued: 1998 • Retired: 1999
Market Value: **7**–$14 **6**–$17

109 ✓

Peter™
8" • Bear • #6084
Issued: 1998 • Retired: 1998
Market Value: **7**–$20 **6**–$24

110 ✓

Piccadilly™
9" • Bear • #6069
Issued: 1998 • Current
A. Multi-Color Striped Suit (1999)
B. "Piccadilly™" Swing Tag/Blue
& Green Suit (1998)
C. "Small Bear" Swing Tag/Blue
& Green Suit (1998)
Market Value: **7**–$_____
6–$18 ("Piccadilly"), $22 ("Small Bear")

111 ✓

Pouncer™
8" • Cat • #6011
Issued: 1994 • Current
A. Bloomers (1998-Current)
B. Sweater (1996-97)
C. Ribbon/Gold & White (1995-96)
D. Ribbon/Gold (1994-95)
Market Value: **7**–$_____ **6**–$16
5–$22 **4**–N/E **3**–$200 **2**–$225
1–$250 (Ribbon/Gold & White),
$235 (Ribbon/Gold)

112

Precious™
12" • Bear • #6104
Issued: 1998 • Retired: 1998
Market Value: **6**–$24

	Date Purchased	Tag Gen.	Price Paid	Value
108.				
109.				
110.				
111.				
112.				

Totals

Attic Treasures™

113

Prince™
7" • Frog • #6048
Issued: 1996 • Retired: 1998
Market Value: ⑥–$18 ⑤–$22

114

Priscilla™
12" • Pig • #6045
Issued: 1996 • Retired: 1997
A. Overalls (1996-97)
B. No Clothes (1996)
Market Value: ⑤–$55

115

Purrcy™
8" • Cat • #6022
Issued: 1995 • Current
A. Bloomers (1998-Current)
B. Overalls (1996-97)
C. Ribbon (1995-96)
Market Value: ⑦–$_____ ⑥–$17
⑤–$26 ④–$105 ③–$130 ②–$175

116

Radcliffe™
9" • Raccoon • #6087
Issued: 1999 • Current
Market Value: ⑦–$_____

Attic Treasures™

	Date Purchased	Tag Gen.	Price Paid	Value
113.				
114.				
115.				
116.				
117.				
			Totals	

117

Rafaella™
8" • Bear • #6066
Issued: 1999 • Current
Market Value: ⑦–$_____

Attic Treasures™

118 ✓

Ramsey™
9" • Ram • #6092
Issued: 1999 • Current
Market Value: ❼–$_____

119

Rebecca™
12" • Bear • #6019
Issued: 1995 • Retired: 1997
A. Overalls (1996-97)
B. Bow (1995-96)
**Market Value: ❺–$66 ❹–$110
❸–$210 ❷–$240**

120

Reggie™
8" • Bear • #6004
Issued: 1993 • Retired: 1995
A. Navy Ribbon (1994-95)
B. Green Ribbon (1994)
C. Red Ribbon (1993)
**Market Value: ❶–$400 (Navy Ribbon),
N/E (Green Ribbon), $515 (Red Ribbon)**

121 ✓

Rosalie™
9" • Bear • #6068
Issued: 1999 • Current
Market Value: ❼–$_____

122

New!

Rosalyne™
8" • Rabbit • #6211
Issued: 2000 • Current
Market Value: ❼–$_____

Attic Treasures™

	Date Purchased	Tag Gen.	Price Paid	Value
118.				
119.				
120.				
121.				
122.				

Totals

Attic Treasures™

123

Rose™
10" • Rabbit • #6078
Issued: 1998 • Retired: 1998
Market Value: ⑦–$16 ⑥–$18

124

Salty™
8" • Bear • #6056
Issued: 1999 • Current
Market Value: ⑦–$_____

125

Samuel™
13" • Bear • #6105
Issued: 1998 • Current
Market Value: ⑦–$_____ ⑥–$16

126

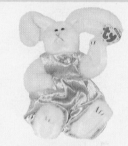

Sara™
12" • Hare • #6007
Issued: 1993 • Retired: 1997
A. Bloomers (1996-97)
B. Ribbon (1993-96)
Market Value: ⑤–$45 ④–$100
③–$145 ②–$200 ①–$255

Attic Treasures™

	Date Purchased	Tag Gen.	Price Paid	Value
123.				
124.				
125.				
126.				
127.				

Totals

127

Sara™
15" • Rabbit • #6120
Issued: 1998 • Retired: 1999
Market Value: ⑦–$15 ⑥–$18

128

Scooter™
9" • Dog • #6032
Issued: 1995 • Retired: 1997
A. Vest (1996-97)
B. No Clothes (1995-96)
Market Value: ⑤–**$44** ④–**$65**
③–**$70** ②–**$90**

129

Scotch™
14" • Bear • #6103
Issued: 1998 • Retired: 1998
Market Value: ⑥–**$26**

130

Scruffy™
9" • Dog • #6085
Issued: 1998 • Retired: 1999
Market Value: ⑦–**$12** ⑥–**$16**

131

Shelby™
9" • Rabbit • #6024
Issued: 1995 • Retired: 1998
A. Dress (1996-98)
B. Ribbon (1995-96)
Market Value: ⑥–**$22** ⑤–**$33**
④–**N/E** ③–**N/E** ②–**$135**

132

Sidney™
15" • Rabbit • #6121
Issued: 1998 • Retired: 1998
Market Value: ⑥–**$23**

	Date Purchased	Tag Gen.	Price Paid	Value
128.				
129.				
130.				
131.				
132.				
Totals				

Attic Treasures™

133

Sire™
13" • Lion • #6141
Issued: 1998 • Retired: 1998
Market Value: 6–$24

134

Skylar™
9" • Bear • #6096
Issued: 1999 • Retired: 1999
Market Value: 7–$18

135

Spencer™
15" • Dog • #6046
Issued: 1996 • Retired: 1997
A. Sweater (1996-97)
B. No Clothes (1996)
Market Value: 5–$43

136

Spruce™
8" • Bear • #6203
Issued: 1999 • Retired: 1999
Market Value: 7–$18

Attic Treasures™

	Date Purchased	Tag Gen.	Price Paid	Value
133.				
134.				
135.				
136.				
137.				

Totals

137

Squeaky™
8" • Mouse • #6017
Issued: 1994 • Retired: 1998
A. No Clothes/Gray & White/Pink Nose &
White Whiskers (1995-98)
B. Ribbon/Gray/Black Nose & Whiskers (1994)
Market Value: 6–$19 5–$25
7–$190 (No Clothes), $200 (Ribbon)

138

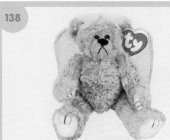

Sterling™
8" • Bear • #6083
Issued: 1998 • Retired: 1999
A. Small Wings (1999)
B. Large Wings (1998)
Market Value: **7**–$20 (Small Wings),
$24 (Large Wings)

139

Strawbunny™
10" • Rabbit • #6079
Issued: 1998 • Retired: 1999
Market Value: **7**–$13 **6**–$16

140

Susannah™
9" • Bear • #6067
Issued: 1999 • Current
Market Value: **7**–$_____

141

Tiny Tim™
8" • Bear • #6001
Issued: 1993 • Retired: 1997
A. Overalls (1996-97)
B. Ribbon (1993-96)
Market Value: **5**–$30 **4**–$65
3–$72 **2**–$115 **1**–$160

142

Tracy™
15" • Dog • #6047
Issued: 1996 • Retired: 1997
A. Overalls (1996-97)
B. No Clothes (1996)
Market Value: **5**–$38

Attic Treasures™

	Date Purchased	Tag Gen.	Price Paid	Value
138.				
139.				
140.				
141.				
142.				

143

Tyler™
12" • Bear • #6002
Issued: 1993 • Retired: 1997
A. Sweater (1996-97)
B. Ribbon (1993-96)
Market Value: ⑤–$43 ④–$75
③–$80 ②–$130 ①–$200

144

Tyra™
8" • Bear • #6201
Issued: 1999 • Retired: 1999
Market Value: ⑦–$975

145

Tyrone™
13" • Bear • #6108
Issued: 1998 • Current
Market Value: ⑦–$_____

146

Waddlesworth™
8" • Penguin • #6202
Issued: 1999 • Current
Market Value: ⑦–$_____

Attic Treasures™

	Date Purchased	Tag Gen.	Price Paid	Value
143.				
144.				
145.				
146.				
147.				

Totals

147

Watson™
14" • Bear • #6065
Issued: 1996 • Retired: 1997
A. Overalls (1996-97)
B. Ribbon (1996)
Market Value: ⑤–$45 (Overalls),
N/E (Ribbon)

148

Wee Willie™
8" • Bear • #6021
Issued: 1995 • Retired: 1997
A. Overalls (1996-97)
B. Ribbon (1995-96)
Market Value: ⑤–$27 ④–$55
③–$60 ②–$120

149

Whiskers™
8" • Cat • #6012
Issued: 1994 • Retired: 1999
A. Bloomers (1998-1999)
B. Overalls (1996-97)
C. Ribbon/Gray & White (1995-96)
D. Ribbon/Gray (1994-95)
Market Value: ⑦–$14 ⑥–$17
⑤–$22 ①–$230 (Ribbon/Gray & White),
$245 (Ribbon/Gray)

150

William™
12" • Bear • #6113
Issued: 1999 • Current
Market Value: ⑦–$_____

151

Woolie™
6" • Bear • #6011
Issued: 1993 • Retired: 1993
Market Value: ①–$1,000

152

Woolie™
6" • Bear • #6012
(appears in the 1993 Ty® catalog,
production not confirmed)
Issued: 1993 • Retired: 1993
Market Value: N/E

Attic Treasures™

	Date Purchased	Tag Gen.	Price Paid	Value
148.				
149.				
150.				
151.				
152.				

Totals

Baby Ty™

In January 2000, Ty Inc. released a new line of cuddly critters called *Baby Ty*. These six baby animals are made of Tylon, an extremely soft material that is also used in the *Beanie Buddies* line. All of the animals in the collection are pastel colored, feature a rattle inside their belly and a heart embroidered on their side. They are infant safe and machine washable, so any one of the huggable animals in this collection is a perfect companion for a little one (although grown-ups are sure to find them irresistible, too). Fans of Ty plush won't want to miss out on this new addition to the family!

1

New!

Bearbaby™
13" • Bear • #3200
Issued: 1/00 • Current
Market Value: $_____

2

New!

Bunnybaby™
13" • Bunny • #3204
Issued: 1/00 • Current
Market Value: $_____

Baby Ty™

	Date Purchased	Price Paid	Value
1.			
2.			
3.			

Totals

3

New!

Dogbaby™
13" • Dog • #3205
Issued: 1/00 • Current
Market Value: $_____

4

New!

Frogbaby™
13" • Frog • #3201
Issued: 1/00 • Current
Market Value: $_____

5

New!

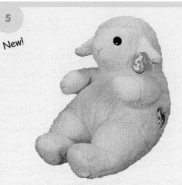

Lamybaby™
13" • Lamb • #3202
Issued: 1/00 • Current
Market Value: $_____

6

New!

Monkeybaby™
13" • Monkey • #3203
Issued: 1/00 • Current
Market Value: $_____

Baby Ty™

	Date Purchased	Price Paid	Value
4.			
5.			
6.			

Totals

Beanie Babies®

What an exciting year for *Beanie Babies!* First came the news on August 31, 1999 that all *Beanie Babies* would be retired by December 31, 1999. Then Ty asked the public to vote via the Internet on whether or not the company should continue producing the popular stuffed animals. After the overwhelmingly favorable results came in, Ty announced that new *Beanie Babies* would be introduced, collectors asked, "When?" That question was partially answered on February 13, 2000, when 20 un-named *Beanie Babies* prototypes went on display at an industry trade show. On March 1, 2000, the animals and their names were unveiled to the public on the Ty Inc. website.

This section provides you with information on all 241 *Beanie Babies* issue dates, birthdates and secondary market values. Additionally, pieces that were promotional giveaways at sporting events are noted.

TAG KEY

- 6 – 6th Generation
- 5 – 5th Generation
- 4 – 4th Generation
- 3 – 3rd Generation
- 2 – 2nd Generation
- 1 – 1st Generation

SPORTS PROMOTION BEANIE BABIES® KEY

Canadian Special Olympics

National Basketball Association

National Hockey League

Major League Baseball

National Football League

Women's National Basketball Association

Beanie Babies®

Date Purchased	Tag Gen.	Price Paid	Value
1.			

Totals

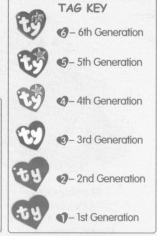

#1 Bear™
(exclusive Ty sales representative gift)
10" • Bear • N/A • Born: N/A
Issued: 12/98 • Not Avail. In Retail Stores
Market Value: Special Tag – **$9,200**

2

1997 Teddy™
10" • Bear • #4200 • Born: 12/25/96
Issued: 10/97 • Retired: 12/97
Market Value: ❹–**$48**

3

1998 Holiday Teddy™
10" • Bear • #4204 • Born: 12/25/98
Issued: 9/98 • Retired: 12/98
Market Value: ❺–**$50**

4

1999 Holiday Teddy™
10" • Bear • #4257 • Born: 12/25/99
Issued: 8/99 • Retired: 12/99
Market Value: ❺–**$35**

5

1999 Signature Bear™
10" • Bear • #4228 • Born: N/A
Issued: 1/99 • Retired: 10/99
Market Value: ❺–**$18**

6

New!

2000 Signature Bear™
10" • Bear • #4266 • Born: N/A
Issued: 2/00 • Current
Market Value: ❻–**$_____**

Beanie Babies®

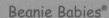

	Date Purchased	Tag Gen.	Price Paid	Value
2.				
3.				
4.				
5.				
6.				

Totals **67**

Beanie Babies®

7

Ally™
12" • Alligator • #4032 • Born: 3/14/94
Issued: 6/94 • Retired: 10/97
Market Value: ④–**$45** ③–**$120**
②–**$260** ①–**$425**

8

Almond™
10" • Bear • #4246 • Born: 4/14/99
Issued: 4/99 • Retired: 12/99
Market Value: ⑤–**$10**

9

Amber™
10" • Cat • #4243 • Born: 2/21/99
Issued: 4/99 • Retired: 12/99
Market Value: ⑤–**$10**

10

Ants™
12" • Anteater • #4195 • Born: 11/7/97
Issued: 5/98 • Retired: 12/98
Market Value: ⑤–**$10**

Beanie Babies®

	Date Purchased	Tag Gen.	Price Paid	Value
7.				
8.				
9.				
10.				
11.				

Totals

11

New!

Aurora™
6" • Polar Bear • #4271 • Born: 2/3/00
Issued: 2/00 • Current
Market Value: ⑥–**$_____**

12

B.B. Bear™
10" • Bear • #4253 • Born: N/A
Issued: Summer 1999 • Retired: 12/99
Market Value: ⑤–**$25**

13

Baldy™
8" • Eagle • #4074 • Born: 2/17/96
Issued: 5/97 • Retired: 5/98
Market Value: ⑤–**$16** ④–**$20**

14

B.

A.

Batty™
5" • Bat • #4035 • Born: 10/29/96
Issued: 10/97 • Retired: 3/99
Market Value:
A. Tie-dye (1/99-3/99) ⑤–**$18**
B. Brown (10/97-1/99) ⑤–**$11** ④–**$12**

15

Beak™
7" • Kiwi • #4211 • Born: 2/3/98
Issued: 9/98 • Retired: 12/99
Market Value: ⑤–**$8**

16

Bernie™
10" • St. Bernard • #4109 • Born: 10/3/96
Issued: 1/97 • Retired: 9/98
Market Value: ⑤–**$12** ④–**$14**

Beanie Babies®

	Date Purchased	Tag Gen.	Price Paid	Value
12.				
13.				
14.				
15.				
16.				

Totals

69

Beanie Babies®

17

Bessie™
10" • Cow • #4009 • Born: 6/27/95
Issued: 6/95 • Retired: 10/97
Market Value: ❹–**$57** ❸–**$115**

18

Billionaire bear™
(exclusive Ty employee gift)
10" • Bear • N/A • Born: N/A
Issued: 9/98 • Not Avail. In Retail Stores
Market Value: Special Tag –**$2,750**

19

Billionaire 2™
(exclusive Ty employee gift)
10" • Bear • N/A • Born: N/A
Issued: 9/99 • Not Avail. In Retail Stores
Market Value: Special Tag –**$5,800**

20

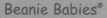

Blackie™
10" • Bear • #4011 • Born: 7/15/94
Issued: 6/94 • Retired: 9/98
Market Value: ❺–**$15** ❹–**$15**
❸–**$82** ❷–**$230** ❶–**$350**

21

Blizzard™
10" • Tiger • #4163 • Born: 12/12/96
Issued: 5/97 • Retired: 5/98
Market Value: ❺–**$16** ❹–**$17**

Beanie Babies®

	Date Purchased	Tag Gen.	Price Paid	Value
17.				
18.				
19.				
20.				
21.				

Totals

22

Bones™
10" • Dog • #4001 • Born: 1/18/94
Issued: 6/94 • Retired: 5/98
Market Value: ⑤–**$17** ④–**$18**
③–**$95** ②–**$230** ①–**$400**

23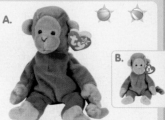
A.

B.

Bongo™
(name changed from "Nana™")
9" • Monkey • #4067 • Born: 8/17/95
Issued: 6/95 • Retired: 12/98
Market Value:
A. Tan Tail (6/95-12/98)
⑤–**$12** ④–**$13** ③–**$130**
B. Brown Tail (2/96-6/96) ④–**$55** ③–**$165**

24

Britannia™
(exclusive to the United Kingdom)
10" • Bear • #4601 • Born: 12/15/97
Issued: 12/97 • Retired: 7/99
Market Value (in U.S. market): ⑤–**$125**

25

Bronty™
7" • Brontosaurus • #4085 • Born: N/A
Issued: 6/95 • Retired: 6/96
Market Value: ③–**$750**

Beanie Babies®

	Date Purchased	Tag Gen.	Price Paid	Value
22.				
23.				
24.				
25.				

Totals

26

Brownie™
(name changed to "Cubbie™")
10" • Bear • #4010 • Born: N/A
Issued: 1/94 • Retired: 1994
Market Value: ①–$3,200

27

Bruno™
10" • Dog • #4183 • Born: 9/9/97
Issued: 12/97 • Retired: 9/98
Market Value: ⑤–$9

28

Bubbles™
8" • Fish • #4078 • Born: 7/2/95
Issued: 6/95 • Retired: 5/97
Market Value: ④–$125 ③–$190

29

Bucky™
11" • Beaver • #4016 • Born: 6/8/95
Issued: 1/96 • Retired: 12/97
Market Value: ④–$32 ③–$90

30

Bumble™
6" • Bee • #4045 • Born: 10/16/95
Issued: 6/95 • Retired: 6/96
Market Value: ④–$485 ③–$450

Beanie Babies®

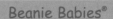

	Date Purchased	Tag Gen.	Price Paid	Value
26.				
27.				
28.				
29.				
30.				

Totals

31

New!

Bushy™
10" • Lion • #4285 • Born: 1/27/00
Issued: 2/00 • Current
Market Value: 6–$_____

32

Butch™
10" • Bull Terrier • #4227 • Born: 10/2/98
Issued: 1/99 • Retired: 12/99
Market Value: 5–$9

33

Canyon™
9" • Cougar • #4212 • Born: 5/29/98
Issued: 9/98 • Retired: 8/99
Market Value: 5–$9

34

Caw™
10" • Crow • #4071 • Born: N/A
Issued: 6/95 • Retired: 6/96
Market Value: 3–$550

35

Cheeks™
10" • Baboon • #4250 • Born: 5/18/99
Issued: 4/99 • Retired: 12/99
Market Value: 5–$11

Beanie Babies®

	Date Purchased	Tag Gen.	Price Paid	Value
31.				
32.				
33.				
34.				
35.				

Totals

36

Chilly™
10" • Polar Bear • #4012 • Born: N/A
Issued: 6/94 • Retired: 1/96
Market Value: ③–**$1,500**
②–**$1,700** ①–**$2,000**

37

Chip™
10" • Cat • #4121 • Born: 1/26/96
Issued: 5/97 • Retired: 3/99
Market Value: ⑤–**$10** ④–**$10**

38

Chipper™
9" • Chipmunk • #4259 • Born: 4/21/99
Issued: 8/99 • Retired: 12/99
Market Value: ⑤–**$11**

39

Chocolate™
10" • Moose • #4015 • Born: 4/27/93
Issued: 1/94 • Retired: 12/98
Market Value: ⑤–**$10** ④–**$10**
③–**$90** ②–**$280** ①–**$520**

40

Chops™
8" • Lamb • #4019 • Born: 5/3/96
Issued: 1/96 • Retired: 1/97
Market Value: ④–**$130** ③–**$200**

Beanie Babies®

	Date Purchased	Tag Gen.	Price Paid	Value
36.				
37.				
38.				
39.				
40.				

Totals

41

Claude™
10" • Crab • #4083 • Born: 9/3/96
Issued: 5/97 • Retired: 12/98
Market Value: ⑤–**$11** ④–**$13**

42

Clubby™
(exclusive to Beanie Babies®
Official Club™ members)
10" • Bear • N/A • Born: 7/7/98
Issued: 5/98 • Retired: 3/99
Market Value: ⑤–**$42**

43

Clubby II™
10" • Bear • N/A • Born: 3/9/99
Issued: 3/99 • Current
Market Value: ⑤–**$30**

44

Congo™
8" • Gorilla • #4160 • Born: 11/9/96
Issued: 6/96 • Retired: 12/98
Market Value: ⑤–**$11** ④–**$12**

Beanie Babies®

	Date Purchased	Tag Gen.	Price Paid	Value
41.				
42.				
43.				
44.				

Totals

45

Coral™
8" • Fish • #4079 • Born: 3/2/95
Issued: 6/95 • Retired: 1/97
Market Value: ④–$150 ③–$215

46

Crunch™
8" • Shark • #4130 • Born: 1/13/96
Issued: 1/97 • Retired: 9/98
Market Value: ⑤–$11 ④–$12

47

Cubbie™
(name changed from "Brownie™")
10" • Bear • #4010 • Born: 11/14/93
Issued: 1/94 • Retired: 12/97
Market Value: ⑤–$22 ④–$30
③–$150 ②–$290 ①–$550

48

Curly™
10" • Bear • #4052 • Born: 4/12/96
Issued: 6/96 • Retired: 12/98
Market Value: ⑤–$20 ④–$22

Beanie Babies®

	Date Purchased	Tag Gen.	Price Paid	Value
45.				
46.				
47.				
48.				
			Totals	

49

Daisy™
10" • Cow • #4006 • Born: 5/10/94
Issued: 6/94 • Retired: 9/98
Market Value: ⑤–**$13** ④–**$15**
③–**$110** ②–**$250** ①–**$370**

50

A.

Derby™
10" • Horse • #4008 • Born: 9/16/95
Issued: 6/95 • Retired: 5/99
Market Value:
A. Star/Fluffy Mane (1/99-5/99)
⑤–**$12**
B. Star/Coarse Mane (12/97-1/99)
⑤–**$13**
C. Coarse Mane (Est. Late 95-12/97)
④–**$20** ③–**$360**
D. Fine Mane (Est. 6/95-Late 95)
③–**$2,250**

B.

C.

D.

51

B.
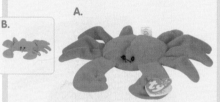

A.

Digger™
10" • Crab • #4027 • Born: 8/23/95
Issued: 6/94 • Retired: 5/97
Market Value:
A. Red (6/95-5/97) ④–**$90** ③–**$175**
B. Orange (6/94-6/95) ③–**$575**
②–**$700** ①–**$850**

52

Doby™
10" • Doberman • #4110 • Born: 10/9/96
Issued: 1/97 • Retired: 12/98
Market Value: ⑤–**$11** ④–**$12**

Beanie Babies®

	Date Purchased	Tag Gen.	Price Paid	Value
49.				
50.				
51.				
52.				

Totals

53

Doodle™
(name changed to "Strut™")
8" • Rooster • #4171 • Born: 3/8/96
Issued: 5/97 • Retired: 1997
Market Value: ④–**$32**

54

Dotty™
10" • Dalmatian • #4100 • Born: 10/17/96
Issued: 5/97 • Retired: 12/98
Market Value: ⑤–**$12** ④–**$13**

55

Early™
8" • Robin • #4190 • Born: 3/20/97
Issued: 5/98 • Retired: 12/99
Market Value: ⑤–**$8**

56

Ears™
9" • Rabbit • #4018 • Born: 4/18/95
Issued: 1/96 • Retired: 5/98
Market Value: ⑤–**$13** ④–**$14** ③–**$75**

57

Echo™
10" • Dolphin • #4180 • Born: 12/21/96
Issued: 5/97 • Retired: 5/98
Market Value: ⑤–**$15** ④–**$17**

Beanie Babies®

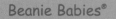

	Date Purchased	Tag Gen.	Price Paid	Value
53.				
54.				
55.				
56.				
57.				
Totals				

58

Eggbert™
8" • Chick • #4232 • Born: 4/10/98
Issued: 1/99 • Retired: 7/99
Market Value: –$13

59

Erin™
10" • Bear • #4186 • Born: 3/17/97
Issued: 1/98 • Retired: 5/99
Market Value: –$20

60

Eucalyptus™
9" • Koala • #4240 • Born: 4/28/99
Issued: 4/99 • Retired: 10/99
Market Value: –$14

61

Ewey™
9" • Lamb • #4219 • Born: 3/1/98
Issued: 1/99 • Retired: 7/99
Market Value: –$12

62

Fetch™
9" • Golden Retriever • #4189 • Born: 2/4/97
Issued: 5/98 • Retired: 12/98
Market Value: –$14

Beanie Babies®

	Date Purchased	Tag Gen.	Price Paid	Value
58.				
59.				
60.				
61.				
62.				

Totals

Beanie Babies®

63

Flash™
10" • Dolphin • #4021 • Born: 5/13/93
Issued: 1/94 • Retired: 5/97
Market Value: ④–**$100** ③–**$165**
②–**$330** ①–**$500**

64

Fleece™
9" • Lamb • #4125 • Born: 3/21/96
Issued: 1/97 • Retired: 12/98
Market Value: ⑤–**$12** ④–**$13**

65

New!

Fleecie™
7" • Lamb • #4279 • Born: 1/26/00
Issued: 2/00 • Current
Market Value: ⑥–$_____

66

Flip™
10" • Cat • #4012 • Born: 2/28/95
Issued: 1/96 • Retired: 10/97
Market Value: ④–**$32** ③–**$90**

Beanie Babies®

	Date Purchased	Tag Gen.	Price Paid	Value
63.				
64.				
65.				
66.				
67.				
			Totals	

67

Flitter™
7" • Butterfly • #4255 • Born: 6/2/99
Issued: Summer 1999 • Retired: 12/99
Market Value: ⑤–**$20**

68

Floppity™
10" • Bunny • #4118 • Born: 5/28/96
Issued: 1/97 • Retired: 5/98
Market Value: ⑤–$17 ④–$18

69

Flutter™
6" • Butterfly • #4043 • Born: N/A
Issued: 6/95 • Retired: 6/96
Market Value: ③–$800

70

Fortune™
10" • Panda • #4196 • Born: 12/6/97
Issued: 5/98 • Retired: 8/99
Market Value: ⑤–$12

71

Freckles™
10" • Leopard • #4066 • Born: 6/3/96 or 7/28/96
Issued: 6/96 • Retired: 12/98
Market Value: ⑤–$12 ④–$13

72

New!

Frigid™
7" • Penguin • #4270 • Born: 1/23/00
Issued: 2/00 • Current
Market Value: ⑥–$_____

Beanie Babies®

	Date Purchased	Tag Gen.	Price Paid	Value
68.				
69.				
70.				
71.				
72.				

Totals

81

Beanie Babies®

Fuzz™
10" • Bear • #4237 • Born: 7/23/98
Issued: 1/99 • Retired: 12/99
Market Value: ⑤–$16

Garcia™
10" • Bear • #4051 • Born: 8/1/95
Issued: 1/96 • Retired: 5/97
Market Value: ④–$165 ③–$250

Germania™
(exclusive to Germany)
10" • Bear • #4236 • Geburtstag: 10/3/98
Issued: 1/99 • Retired: 12/99
Market Value (in U.S. market): ⑤–$190

GiGi™
8" • Poodle • #4191 • Born: 4/7/97
Issued: 5/98 • Retired: 12/99
Market Value: ⑤–$8

Beanie Babies®

	Date Purchased	Tag Gen.	Price Paid	Value
73.				
74.				
75.				
76.				
77.				

Totals

Glory™
10" • Bear • #4188 • Born: 7/4/97
Issued: 5/98 • Retired: 12/98
Market Value: ⑤–$36

78

New!

Glow™
7" • Lightning Bug • #4283 • Born: 1/4/00
Issued: 2/00 • Current
Market Value: *6*–$_____

79

Goatee™
8" • Mountain Goat • #4235 • Born: 11/4/98
Issued: 1/99 • Retired: 12/99
Market Value: *5*–$9

80

Gobbles™
8" • Turkey • #4034 • Born: 11/27/96
Issued: 10/97 • Retired: 3/99
Market Value: *5*–$10 *4*–$12

81

Goldie™
8" • Goldfish • #4023 • Born: 11/14/94
Issued: 6/94 • Retired: 12/97
Market Value: *5*–$38 *4*–$38
3–$105 *2*–$260 *1*–$430

82

Goochy™
10" • Jellyfish • #4230 • Born: 11/18/98
Issued: 1/99 • Retired: 12/99
Market Value: *5*–$10

Beanie Babies®

	Date Purchased	Tag Gen.	Price Paid	Value
78.				
79.				
80.				
81.				
82.				

Totals

Beanie Babies®

83

New!

Grace™
7" • Bunny • #4274 • Born: 2/10/00
Issued: 2/00 • Current
Market Value: ⑥-$_____

84

Gracie™
8" • Swan • #4126 • Born: 6/17/96
Issued: 1/97 • Retired: 5/98
Market Value: ⑤-$14   ④-$15

85

Groovy™
10" • Bear • #4256 • Born: 1/10/99
Issued: 8/99 • Retired: 12/99
Market Value: ⑤-$27

86

Grunt™
10" • Razorback • #4092 • Born: 7/19/95
Issued: 1/96 • Retired: 5/97
Market Value: ④-$130   ③-$185

Beanie Babies®

	Date Purchased	Tag Gen.	Price Paid	Value
83.				
84.				
85.				
86.				
87.				

Totals

87

Halo™
10" • Angel Bear • #4208 • Born: 8/31/98
Issued: 9/98 • Retired: 11/99
Market Value: ⑤-$16

88 New!

Halo II™
10" • Angel Bear • #4269 • Born: 1/14/00
Issued: 2/00 • Current
Market Value: ⑥–$____

89

A.

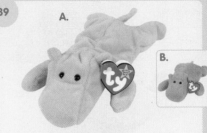

B.

Happy™
10" • Hippo • #4061 • Born: 2/25/94
Issued: 6/94 • Retired: 5/98
Market Value:
A. Lavender (6/95-5/98)
⑤–$22 ④–$24 ③–$180
B. Gray (6/94-6/95)
③–$520 ②–$620 ①–$785

90

Hippie™
10" • Bunny • #4218 • Born: 5/4/98
Issued: 1/99 • Retired: 7/99
Market Value: ⑤–$22

91

Hippity™
10" • Bunny • #4119 • Born: 6/1/96
Issued: 1/97 • Retired: 5/98
Market Value: ⑤–$20 ④–$22

92

Hissy™
25" • Snake • #4185 • Born: 4/4/97
Issued: 12/97 • Retired: 3/99
Market Value: ⑤–$9

Beanie Babies®

	Date Purchased	Tag Gen.	Price Paid	Value
88.				
89.				
90.				
91.				
92.				

Totals

93

Honks™
8" • Goose • #4258 • Born: 3/11/99
Issued: 8/99 • Retired: 12/99
Market Value: ⑤–$10

94

Hoot™
6" • Owl • #4073 • Born: 8/9/95
Issued: 1/96 • Retired: 10/97
Market Value: ④–$38 ③–$105

95

Hope™
9" • Bear • #4213 • Born: 3/23/98
Issued: 1/99 • Retired: 12/99
Market Value: ⑤–$14

96

Hoppity™
10" • Bunny • #4117 • Born: 4/3/96
Issued: 1/97 • Retired: 5/98
Market Value: ⑤–$17 ④–$18

Beanie Babies®

	Date Purchased	Tag Gen.	Price Paid	Value
93.				
94.				
95.				
96.				
97.				
Totals				

97

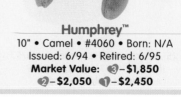

Humphrey™
10" • Camel • #4060 • Born: N/A
Issued: 6/94 • Retired: 6/95
Market Value: ③–$1,850
②–$2,050 ①–$2,450

98

A.

B.

C.

Iggy™
10" • Iguana • #4038 • Born: 8/12/97
Issued: 12/97 • Retired: 3/99
Market Value:
A. Blue/No Tongue (Mid 98-3/99)
⑤–**$11**
B. Tie-dye/With Tongue (6/98-Mid 98)
⑤–**$11**
C. Tie-dye/No Tongue (12/97-6/98)
⑤–**$11**

99

A.

B.

Inch™
12" • Inchworm • #4044 • Born: 9/3/95
Issued: 6/95 • Retired: 5/98
Market Value:
A. Yarn Antennas (10/97-5/98)
⑤–**$23** ④–**$26**
B. Felt Antennas (6/95-10/97)
④–**$150** ③–**$165**

100

A.

B.

C.

Inky™
8" • Octopus • #4028 • Born: 11/29/94
Issued: 6/94 • Retired: 5/98
Market Value:
A. Pink (6/95-5/98)
⑤–**$24** ④–**$28** ③–**$185**
B. Tan/With Mouth (9/94-6/95)
③–**$625** ②–**$700**
C. Tan/No Mouth (6/94-9/94)
②–**$750** ①–**$915**

101

Jabber™
10" • Parrot • #4197 • Born: 10/10/97
Issued: 5/98 • Retired: 12/99
Market Value: ⑤–**$8**

102

Jake™
9" • Mallard Duck • #4199 • Born: 4/16/97
Issued: 5/98 • Retired: 12/99
Market Value: ⑤–**$8**

Beanie Babies®

	Date Purchased	Tag Gen.	Price Paid	Value
98.				
99.				
100.				
101.				
102.				

Totals

Beanie Babies®

103

Jolly™
10" • Walrus • #4082 • Born: 12/2/96
Issued: 5/97 • Retired: 5/98
Market Value: ⑤−$14 ④−$15

104

Kicks™
10" • Bear • #4229 • Born: 8/16/98
Issued: 1/99 • Retired: 12/99
Market Value: ⑤−$14

105

Kiwi™
10" • Toucan • #4070 • Born: 9/16/95
Issued: 6/95 • Retired: 1/97
Market Value: ④−$145 ③−$220

106

Knuckles™
9" • Pig • #4247 • Born: 3/25/99
Issued: 4/99 • Retired: 12/99
Market Value: ⑤−$13

Beanie Babies®

	Date Purchased	Tag Gen.	Price Paid	Value
103.				
104.				
105.				
106.				
107.				

Totals

107

KuKu™
10" • Cockatoo • #4192 • Born: 1/5/97
Issued: 5/98 • Retired: 12/99
Market Value: ⑤−$8

108

Lefty™
8" • Donkey • #4085 • Born: 7/4/96
Issued: 6/96 • Retired: 1/97
Market Value: ④-$235

109

Legs™
10" • Frog • #4020 • Born: 4/25/93
Issued: 1/94 • Retired: 10/97
Market Value: ④-$20 ③-$88
②-$310 ①-$480

110

Libearty™
10" • Bear • #4057 • Born: Summer 1996
Issued: 6/96 • Retired: 1/97
Market Value: ④-$365

111

Lips™
7" • Fish • #4254 • Born: 3/15/99
Issued: Summer 1999 • Retired: 12/99
Market Value: ⑤-$18

Beanie Babies®

	Date Purchased	Tag Gen.	Price Paid	Value
108.				
109.				
110.				
111.				

Totals

Beanie Babies®

112

A.

B.

Lizzy™
12" • Lizard • #4033 • Born: 5/11/95
Issued: 6/95 • Retired: 12/97
Market Value:
A. Blue (1/96-12/97)
⑤–**$22**   ④–**$24**   ③–**$205**
B. Tie-dye (6/95-1/96) ③–**$835**

113

Loosy™
8" • Goose • #4206 • Born: 3/29/98
Issued: 9/98 • Retired: 9/99
Market Value: ⑤–**$10**

114

A.

B.

C.

Lucky™
6" • Ladybug • #4040 • Born: 5/1/95
Issued: 6/94 • Retired: 5/98
Market Value:
A. Approx. 11 Printed Spots
(2/96-5/98) ⑤–**$23**   ④–**$23**
B. Approx. 21 Printed Spots
(Est. Mid 96-Late 96) ④–**$390**
C. Approx. 7 Felt Glued-On Spots
(6/94-2/96) ③–**$215**
②–**$390**   ①–**$590**

115

Luke™
10" • Black Lab • #4214 • Born: 6/15/98
Issued: 1/99 • Retired: 12/99
Market Value: ⑤–**$11**

Beanie Babies®

	Date Purchased	Tag Gen.	Price Paid	Value
112.				
113.				
114.				
115.				
116.				

Totals

116

Mac™
9" • Cardinal • #4225 • Born: 6/10/98
Issued: 1/99 • Retired: 12/99
Market Value: ⑤–**$11**

117

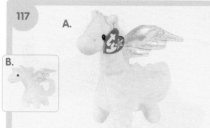

Magic™
10" • Dragon • #4088 • Born: 9/5/95
Issued: 6/95 • Retired: 12/97
Market Value:
A. Pale Pink Thread (6/95-12/97)
④–**$46** ③–**$125**
B. Hot Pink Thread (Est. Mid 96-Early 97)
④–**$80**

118

Manny™
9" • Manatee • #4081 • Born: 6/8/95
Issued: 1/96 • Retired: 5/97
Market Value: ④–**$125** ③–**$200**

119

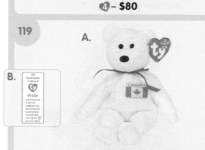

Maple™
(exclusive to Canada)
10" • Bear • #4600 • Born: 7/1/96
Issued: 1/97 • Retired: 7/99
Market Value (in U.S. market):
A. "Maple™" Tush Tag (Est. Early 97-7/99)
⑤–**$140** ④–**$170**
B. "Pride™" Tush Tag (Est. Early 97) ④–**$450**

120

Mel™
8" • Koala • #4162 • Born: 1/15/96
Issued: 1/97 • Retired: 3/99
Market Value: ⑤–**$9** ④–**$10**

121

Millennium™
10" • Bear • #4226 • Born: 1/1/99
Issued: 1/99 • Retired: 11/99
Market Value: A. "Millennium™"
On Both Tags (Early 99-11/99)
⑤–**$13**
B. "Millenium™" Swing Tag &
"Millennium™" Tush Tag (Early 99)
⑤–**$25**
C. "Millenium™" On Both Tags
(1/99-Early 99) ⑤–**$21**

Beanie Babies®

	Date Purchased	Tag Gen.	Price Paid	Value
117.				
118.				
119.				
120.				
121.				

Totals

91

Beanie Babies®

122

Mooch™
9" • Spider Monkey • #4224 • Born: 8/1/98
Issued: 1/99 • Retired: 12/99
Market Value: *5*–**$10**

123

New!

Morrie™
14" • Eel • #4282 • Born: 2/20/00
Issued: 2/00 • Current
Market Value: *6*–$_____

124

A.

B.

C.

D.

Mystic™
10" • Unicorn • #4007 • Born: 5/21/94
Issued: 6/94 • Retired: 5/99
Market Value:
A. Iridescent Horn/Fluffy Mane
(1/99-5/99) *5*–**$14**
B. Iridescent Horn/Coarse Mane
(10/97-12/98) *5*–**$11** *4*–**$12**
C. Brown Horn/Coarse Mane
(Est. Late 95-10/97) *4*–**$25** *3*–**$100**
D. Brown Horn/Fine Mane
(Est. 6/94-Late 95) *3*–**$295**
2–**$460** *1*–**$550**

125

Nana™
(name changed to "Bongo™")
9" • Monkey • #4067 • Born: N/A
Issued: 6/95 • Retired: 1995
Market Value: *3*–**$3,700**

Beanie Babies®

	Date Purchased	Tag Gen.	Price Paid	Value
122.				
123.				
124.				
125.				
126.				
Totals				

126

Nanook™
10" • Husky • #4104 • Born: 11/21/96
Issued: 5/97 • Retired: 3/99
Market Value: *5*–**$11** *4*–**$12**

127

Neon™
10" • Seahorse • #4239 • Born: 4/1/99
Issued: 4/99 • Retired: 12/99
Market Value: ⑤–**$12**

128

Nibbler™
8" • Rabbit • #4216 • Born: 4/6/98
Issued: 1/99 • Retired: 7/99
Market Value: ⑤–**$13**

129

Nibbly™
8" • Rabbit • #4217 • Born: 5/7/98
Issued: 1/99 • Retired: 7/99
Market Value: ⑤–**$12**

130

New!

Niles™
9" • Camel • #4284 • Born: 2/1/00
Issued: 2/00 • Current
Market Value: ⑥–$_____

131

A.

B.

C.

Nip™
10" • Cat • #4003 • Born: 3/6/94
Issued: 1/95 • Retired: 12/97
Market Value:
A. White Paws (3/96-12/97)
⑤–**$18** ④–**$18** ③–**$250**
B. All Gold (1/96-3/96) ③–**$840**
C. White Face (1/95-1/96)
③–**$480** ②–**$540**

	Beanie Babies®		
	Date Purchased	Tag Gen.	Price Paid	Value
127.				
128.				
129.				
130.				
131.				

Totals

132

Nuts™
8" • Squirrel • #4114 • Born: 1/21/96
Issued: 1/97 • Retired: 12/98
Market Value: ⑤–$11 ④–$13

133

Osito™
(exclusive to the United States)
10" • Bear • #4244 • Born: 2/5/99
Issued: 4/99 • Retired: 11/99
Market Value: ⑤–$25

134

A.

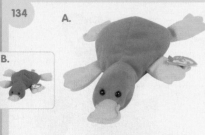

B.

Patti™
10" • Platypus • #4025 • Born: 1/6/93
Issued: 1/94 • Retired: 5/98
Market Value:
A. Magenta (2/95-5/98) ⑤–$17
④–$21 ③–$210
B. Maroon (1/94-2/95) ③–$650
②–$800 ①–$900

135

Paul™
10" • Walrus • #4248 • Born: 2/23/99
Issued: 4/99 • Retired: 12/99
Market Value: ⑤–$12

136

Peace™
10" • Bear • #4053 • Born: 2/1/96
Issued: 5/97 • Retired: 7/99
Market Value: ⑤–$21 ④–$27

Beanie Babies®

	Date Purchased	Tag Gen.	Price Paid	Value
132.				
133.				
134.				
135.				
136.				

Totals

137

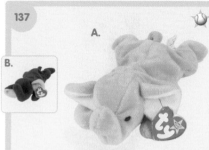

A.

B.

Peanut™
10" • Elephant • #4062 • Born: 1/25/95
Issued: 6/95 • Retired: 5/98
Market Value:
A. Light Blue (10/95-5/98) ⑤–**$20**
④–**$23** ③–**$750**
B. Dark Blue (6/95-10/95) ③–**$4,400**

138

Pecan™
10" • Bear • #4251 • Born: 4/15/99
Issued: 4/99 • Retired: 12/99
Market Value: ⑤–**$11**

139

Peking™
10" • Panda • #4013 • Born: N/A
Issued: 6/94 • Retired: 1/96
Market Value: ③–**$1,600**
②–**$1,700** ①–**$2,150**

140

A.

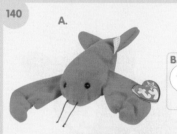

B.

Pinchers™
10" • Lobster • #4026 • Born: 6/19/93
Issued: 1/94 • Retired: 5/98
Market Value:
A. "Pinchers™" Swing Tag (1/94-5/98) ⑤–**$19**
④–**$20** ③–**$105** ②–**$390** ①–**$800**
B. "Punchers™" Swing Tag (Est. Early 94)
①–**$3,500**

Beanie Babies®

	Date Purchased	Tag Gen.	Price Paid	Value
137.				
138.				
139.				
140.				

Totals

Beanie Babies®

141

Pinky™
10" • Flamingo • #4072 • Born: 2/13/95
Issued: 6/95 • Retired: 12/98
Market Value: ⑤–$10 ④–$12
③–$115

142

Pouch™
8" • Kangaroo • #4161 • Born: 11/6/96
Issued: 1/97 • Retired: 3/99
Market Value: ⑤–$9 ④–$11

143

Pounce™
10" • Cat • #4122 • Born: 8/28/97
Issued: 12/97 • Retired: 3/99
Market Value: ⑤–$9

144

Prance™
10" • Cat • #4123 • Born: 11/20/97
Issued: 12/97 • Retired: 3/99
Market Value: ⑤–$9

Beanie Babies®

	Date Purchased	Tag Gen.	Price Paid	Value
141.				
142.				
143.				
144.				
145.				
Totals				

145

Prickles™
5" • Hedgehog • #4220 • Born: 2/19/98
Issued: 1/99 • Retired: 12/99
Market Value: ⑤–$10

146

A.

B.

Princess™
10" • Bear • #4300 • Born: N/A
Issued: 10/97 • Retired: 4/99
Market Value:
A. "P.E. Pellets" On Tush Tag
(Est. Late 97-4/99) ④–**$23**
B. "P.V.C. Pellets" On Tush Tag
(Est. Late 97) ④–**$95**

147

Puffer™
9" • Puffin • #4181 • Born: 11/3/97
Issued: 12/97 • Retired: 9/98
Market Value: ⑤–**$10**

148

Pugsly™
10" • Pug Dog • #4106 • Born: 5/2/96
Issued: 5/97 • Retired: 3/99
Market Value: ⑤–**$10** ④–**$11**

149

Pumkin'™
9" • Pumpkin • #4205 • Born: 10/31/98
Issued: 9/98 • Retired: 12/98
Market Value: ⑤–**$25**

Beanie Babies®

	Date Purchased	Tag Gen.	Price Paid	Value
146.				
147.				
148.				
149.				

Totals

97

Beanie Babies®

150

B.

Quackers™
8" • Duck • #4024 • Born: 4/19/94
Issued: 6/94 • Retired: 5/98
Market Value:
A. "Quackers™" With Wings (1/95-5/98)
⑤–**$13**   ④–**$15**   ③–**$85**   ②–**$600**
B. "Quacker™" Without Wings (6/94-1/95)
②–**$1,900**   ①–**$2,300**

151

Radar™
6" • Bat • #4091 • Born: 10/30/95
Issued: 9/95 • Retired: 5/97
Market Value: ④–**$130**   ③–**$195**

152

Rainbow™
10" • Chameleon • #4037 • Born: 10/14/97
Issued: 12/97 • Retired: 3/99
Market Value:
A. Tie-dye/With Tongue (Mid 98-3/99)
⑤–**$13**
B. Blue/No Tongue (12/97-Mid 98)   ⑤–**$13**

153

Rex™
7" • Tyrannosaurus • #4086 • Born: N/A
Issued: 6/95 • Retired: 6/96
Market Value: ③–**$700**

Beanie Babies®

	Date Purchased	Tag Gen.	Price Paid	Value
150.				
151.				
152.				
153.				
	Totals			

154

Righty™
10" • Elephant • #4086 • Born: 7/4/96
Issued: 6/96 • Retired: 1/97
Market Value: ④–**$235**

155

Ringo™
12" • Raccoon • #4014 • Born: 7/14/95
Issued: 1/96 • Retired: 9/98
Market Value: ⑤–**$12** ④–**$14** ③–**$80**

156

Roam™
8" • Buffalo • #4209 • Born: 9/27/98
Issued: 9/98 • Retired: 12/99
Market Value: ⑤–**$9**

157

Roary™
10" • Lion • #4069 • Born: 2/20/96
Issued: 5/97 • Retired: 12/98
Market Value: ⑤–**$11** ④–**$12**

158

Rocket™
9" • Blue Jay • #4202 • Born: 3/12/97
Issued: 5/98 • Retired: 12/99
Market Value: ⑤–**$8**

Beanie Babies®

	Date Purchased	Tag Gen.	Price Paid	Value
154.				
155.				
156.				
157.				
158.				

Totals

Beanie Babies®

159

Rover™
8" • Dog • #4101 • Born: 5/30/96
Issued: 6/96 • Retired: 5/98
Market Value: ⑤-$19 ④-$21

160

New!

Rufus™
7" • Dog • #4280 • Born: 2/28/00
Issued: 2/00 • Current
Market Value: ⑥-$_____

161

Sammy™
10" • Bear • #4215 • Born: 6/23/98
Issued: 1/99 • Retired: 12/99
Market Value: ⑤-$11

162

Santa™
9" • Elf • #4203 • Born: 12/6/98
Issued: 9/98 • Retired: 12/98
Market Value: ⑤-$30

Beanie Babies®

	Date Purchased	Tag Gen.	Price Paid	Value
159.				
160.				
161.				
162.				
163.				

Totals

163

New!

Sakura™
(exclusive to Japan)
10" • Bear • #4602 • Born: 3/25/00
Issued: 3/00 • Current
Market Value: ⑥-$_____

164

New!

Sarge™
8" • German Shepherd • #4277 • Born: 2/14/00
Issued: 2/00 • Current
Market Value: ⑥–$_____

165

Scaly™
10" • Lizard • #4263 • Born: 2/9/99
Issued: 8/99 • Retired: 12/99
Market Value: ⑤–$10

166

Scat™
10" • Cat • #4231 • Born: 5/27/98
Issued: 1/99 • Retired: 12/99
Market Value: ⑤–$10

167

Schweetheart™
10" • Orangutan • #4252 • Born: 1/23/99
Issued: 4/99 • Retired: 12/99
Market Value: ⑤–$11

168

Scoop™
8" • Pelican • #4107 • Born: 7/1/96
Issued: 6/96 • Retired: 12/98
Market Value: ⑤–$11 ④–$12

Beanie Babies®

	Date Purchased	Tag Gen.	Price Paid	Value
164.				
165.				
166.				
167.				
168.				

Totals

Beanie Babies®

169

Scorch™
11" • Dragon • #4210 • Born: 7/31/98
Issued: 9/98 • Retired: 12/99
Market Value: ⑤–**$10**

170

Scottie™
8" • Scottish Terrier • #4102
Born: 6/3/96 or 6/15/96
Issued: 6/96 • Retired: 5/98
Market Value: ⑤–**$21** ④–**$23**

171

New!

Scurry™
7" • Beetle • #4281 • Born: 1/18/00
Issued: 2/00 • Current
Market Value: ⑥–**$_____**

172

Seamore™
8" • Seal • #4029 • Born: 12/14/96
Issued: 6/94 • Retired: 10/97
Market Value: ④–**$110** ③–**$185**
②–**$400** ①–**$620**

Beanie Babies®

	Date Purchased	Tag Gen.	Price Paid	Value
169.				
170.				
171.				
172.				
173.				

Totals

173

Seaweed™
8" • Otter • #4080 • Born: 3/19/96
Issued: 1/96 • Retired: 9/98
Market Value: ⑤–**$20** ④–**$23** ③–**$85**

174

Sheets™
8" • Ghost • #4260 • Born: 10/31/99
Issued: 8/99 • Retired: 12/99
Market Value: ⑤–$12

175

Silver™
10" • Cat • #4242 • Born: 2/11/99
Issued: 4/99 • Retired: 12/99
Market Value: ⑤–$11

176

Slippery™
10" • Seal • #4222 • Born: 1/17/98
Issued: 1/99 • Retired: 12/99
Market Value: ⑤–$9

177

Slither™
23" • Snake • #4031 • Born: N/A
Issued: 6/94 • Retired: 6/95
Market Value: ③–$1,550
②–$1,750 ①–$2,050

178

Slowpoke™
10" • Sloth • #4261 • Born: 5/20/99
Issued: 8/99 • Retired: 12/99
Market Value: ⑤–$10

Beanie Babies®

	Date Purchased	Tag Gen.	Price Paid	Value
174.				
175.				
176.				
177.				
178.				
			Totals	

179

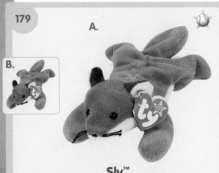

A.

B.

Sly™
10" • Fox • #4115 • Born: 9/12/96
Issued: 6/96 • Retired: 9/98
Market Value:
A. White Belly (8/96-9/98) ⑤–**$12** ④–**$14**
B. Brown Belly (6/96-8/96) ④–**$130**

180

Smoochy™
10" • Frog • #4039 • Born: 10/1/97
Issued: 12/97 • Retired: 3/99
Market Value: ⑤–**$10**

181

New!

Sneaky™
11" • Leopard • #4278 • Born: 2/22/00
Issued: 2/00 • Current
Market Value: ⑥–**$_____**

182

Snip™
10" • Siamese Cat • #4120 • Born: 10/22/96
Issued: 1/97 • Retired: 12/98
Market Value: ⑤–**$11** ④–**$12**

183

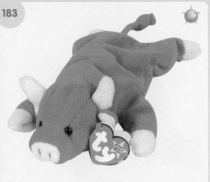

Snort™
10" • Bull • #4002 • Born: 5/15/95
Issued: 1/97 • Retired: 9/98
Market Value: ⑤–**$12** ④–**$13**

Beanie Babies®

	Date Purchased	Tag Gen.	Price Paid	Value
179.				
180.				
181.				
182.				
183.				

Totals

184

Snowball™
8" • Snowman • #4201 • Born: 12/22/96
Issued: 10/97 • Retired: 12/97
Market Value: ④–**$36**

185

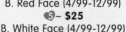

Spangle™
10" • Bear • #4245 • Born: 6/14/99
Issued: 4/99 • Retired: 12/99
Market Value:
A. Blue Face (4/99-12/99) ⑤– **$48**
B. Red Face (4/99-12/99)
⑤– **$25**
B. White Face (4/99-12/99)
⑤–**$35**

186

Sparky™
10" • Dalmatian • #4100 • Born: 2/27/96
Issued: 6/96 • Retired: 5/97
Market Value: ④–**$115**

187

Speedy™
7" • Turtle • #4030 • Born: 8/14/94
Issued: 6/94 • Retired: 10/97
Market Value: ④–**$28** ③–**$95**
②–**$280** ①–**$480**

188

Spike™
10" • Rhinoceros • #4060 • Born: 8/13/96
Issued: 6/96 • Retired: 12/98
Market Value: ⑤–**$9** ④–**$10**

Beanie Babies®

	Date Purchased	Tag Gen.	Price Paid	Value
184.				
185.				
186.				
187.				
188.				

Totals

Beanie Babies®

189

Spinner™
8" • Spider • #4036 • Born: 10/28/96
Issued: 10/97 • Retired: 9/98
Market Value:
A. "Spinner™" Tush Tag (10/97-9/98)
⑤–**$11** ④–**$13**
B. "Creepy™" Tush Tag (Est. Late 97-9/98)
⑤–**$65**

190

Splash™
10" • Whale • #4022 • Born: 7/8/93
Issued: 1/94 • Retired: 5/97
Market Value: ④–**$110** ③–**$160**
②–**$380** ①–**$575**

191

Spooky™
8" • Ghost • #4090 • Born: 10/31/95
Issued: 9/95 • Retired: 12/97
Market Value:
A. "Spooky™" Swing Tag (Est. Late 95-12/97)
④–**$29** ③–**$125**
B. "Spook™" Swing Tag (Est. 9/95-Late 95)
③–**$455**

192

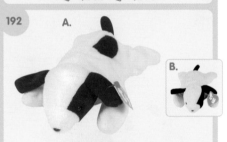

Spot™
10" • Dog • #4000 • Born: 1/3/93
Issued: 1/94 • Retired: 10/97
Market Value:
A. With Spot (4/94-10/97)
④–**$48** ③–**$125** ②–**$650**
B. Without Spot (1/94-4/94)
②–**$1,750** ①–**$2,250**

Beanie Babies®

	Date Purchased	Tag Gen.	Price Paid	Value
189.				
190.				
191.				
192.				

Totals

106

193

New!

Springy™
9" • Bunny • #4272 • Born: 2/29/00
Issued: 2/00 • Current
Market Value: ⑥–$_____

194

Spunky™
10" • Cocker Spaniel • #4184 • Born: 1/14/97
Issued: 12/97 • Retired: 3/99
Market Value: ⑤–$10

195

Squealer™
10" • Pig • #4005 • Born: 4/23/93
Issued: 1/94 • Retired: 5/98
Market Value: ⑤–$24 ④–$26 ③–$82
②–$270 ①–$540

196

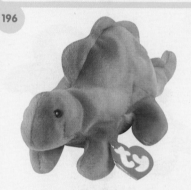

Steg™
9" • Stegosaurus • #4087 • Born: N/A
Issued: 6/95 • Retired: 6/96
Market Value: ③–$750

197

Stilts™
12" • Stork • #4221 • Born: 6/16/98
Issued: 1/99 • Retired: 5/99
Market Value: ⑤–$10

Beanie Babies®

	Date Purchased	Tag Gen.	Price Paid	Value
193.				
194.				
195.				
196.				
197.				

Totals

198

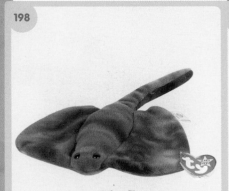

Sting™
10" • Stingray • #4077 • Born: 8/27/95
Issued: 6/95 • Retired: 1/97
Market Value: 4 –**$140** 3 –**$235**

199

Stinger™
12" • Scorpion • #4193 • Born: 9/29/97
Issued: 5/98 • Retired: 12/98
Market Value: 5 –**$10**

200

Stinky™
10" • Skunk • #4017 • Born: 2/13/95
Issued: 6/95 • Retired: 9/98
Market Value: 5 –**$13** 4 –**$15** 3 –**$85**

201

Stretch™
12" • Ostrich • #4182 • Born: 9/21/97
Issued: 12/97 • Retired: 3/99
Market Value: 5 –**$11**

Beanie Babies®

	Date Purchased	Tag Gen.	Price Paid	Value
198.				
199.				
200.				
201.				
202.				

Totals

202

A.

B.

C.

Stripes™
10" • Tiger • #4065 • Born: 6/11/95
Issued: Est. 6/95 • Retired: 5/98
Market Value:
A. Light w/Fewer Stripes
(6/96-5/98) 5 –**$14** 4 –**$16**
B. Dark w/Fuzzy Belly
(Est. Early 96-6/96) 3 –**$800**
C. Dark w/More Stripes
(Est. 6/95-Early 96) 3 –**$375**

203

Strut™
(name changed from "Doodle™")
8" • Rooster • #4171 • Born: 3/8/96
Issued: 7/97 • Retired: 3/99
Market Value: ⑤–**$10** ④–**$12**

204

New!

Swampy™
12" • Alligator • #4273 • Born: 1/24/00
Issued: 2/00 • Current
Market Value: ⑥–$_____

205

Swirly™
8" • Snail • #4249 • Born: 3/10/99
Issued: 4/99 • Retired: 12/99
Market Value: ⑤–**$12**

206

New!

Swoop™
5" • Pterodactyl • #4268 • Born: 2/24/00
Issued: 2/00 • Current
Market Value: ⑥–$_____

207

Tabasco™
10" • Bull • #4002 • Born: 5/15/95
Issued: 6/95 • Retired: 1/97
Market Value: ④–**$140** ③–**$210**

Beanie Babies®

	Date Purchased	Tag Gen.	Price Paid	Value
203.				
204.				
205.				
206.				
207.				

Totals

Beanie Babies®

208

A.

B.

C.

Tank™
9" • Armadillo • #4031 • Born: 2/22/95
Issued: Est. 1/96 • Retired: 10/97
Market Value:
A. 9 Plates/With Shell
(Est. Late 96-10/97) ④–**$65**
B. 9 Plates/Without Shell
(Est. Mid 96-Late 96) ④–**$280**
C. 7 Plates/Without Shell
(Est. 1/96-Mid 96) ③–**$195**

209

A.

B.

Teddy™ (brown)
10" • Bear • #4050 • Born: 11/28/95
Issued: 6/94 • Retired: 10/97
Market Value:
A. New Face (1/95-10/97) ④–**$90**
③–**$350** ②–**$775**
B. Old Face (6/94-1/95) ②–**$2,300** ①–**$2,500**

210

A.

B.

Teddy™ (cranberry)
10" • Bear • #4052 • Born: N/A
Issued: 6/94 • Retired: 1/96
Market Value:
A. New Face (1/95-1/96) ③–**$1,600** ②–**$1,800**
B. Old Face (6/94-1/95) ②–**$1,600** ①–**$1,800**

211

A.

B.

Teddy™ (jade)
10" • Bear • #4057 • Born: N/A
Issued: 6/94 • Retired: 1/96
Market Value:
A. New Face (1/95-1/96) ③–**$1,600** ②–**$1,800**
B. Old Face (6/94-1/95) ②–**$1,600** ①–**$1,800**

Beanie Babies®

	Date Purchased	Tag Gen.	Price Paid	Value
208.				
209.				
210.				
211.				
212.				

Totals

212

A.

B.

Teddy™ (magenta)
10" • Bear • #4056 • Born: N/A
Issued: 6/94 • Retired: 1/96
Market Value:
A. New Face (1/95-1/96) ③–**$1,600** ②–**$1,800**
B. Old Face (6/94-1/95) ②–**$1,600** ①–**$1,800**

213

A.

B.

Teddy™ (teal)
10" • Bear • # 4051 • Born: N/A
Issued: 6/94 • Retired: 1/96
Market Value:
A. New Face (1/95-1/96) ❸–**$1,600** ❷–**$1,800**
B. Old Face (6/94-1/95) ❷–**$1,600** ❶–**$1,800**

214

A.

B.

C.

Teddy™ (violet)
10" • Bear • #4055 • Born: N/A
Issued: 6/94 • Retired: 1/96
Market Value:
A. New Face (1/95-1/96)
❸–**$1,600** ❷–**$1,800**
B. New Face/Employee Bear w/Red
Tush Tag (Green or Red Ribbon)
No Swing Tag – **$3,800**
C. Old Face (6/94-1/95)
❷–**$1,600** ❶–**$1,800**

215

New!

The Beginning™
10" • Bear • #4267 • Born: 1/1/00
Issued: 2/00 • Current
Market Value: ❻–$_____

216

The End™
10" • Bear • #4265 • Born: N/A
Issued: 8/99 • Retired: 12/99
Market Value: ❺–**$40**

217

Tiny™
8" • Chihuahua • #4234 • Born: 9/8/98
Issued: 1/99 • Retired: 12/99
Market Value: ❺–**$11**

Beanie Babies®

	Date Purchased	Tag Gen.	Price Paid	Value
213.				
214.				
215.				
216.				
217.				

Totals

111

Beanie Babies®

218

Tiptoe™
11" • Mouse • #4241 • Born: 1/8/99
Issued: 4/99 • Retired: 10/99
Market Value: ⑤-**$12**

219

Tracker™
9" • Basset Hound • #4198 • Born: 6/5/97
Issued: 5/98 • Retired: 11/99
Market Value: ⑤-**$9**

220

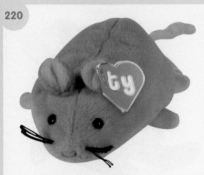

Trap™
9" • Mouse • #4042 • Born: N/A
Issued: 6/94 • Retired: 6/95
Market Value: ③-**$1,150**
②-**$1,450** ①-**$1,750**

221

New!

Trumpet™
9" • Elephant • #4276 • Born: 2/11/00
Issued: 2/00 • Current
Market Value: ⑥-**$____**

Beanie Babies®

	Date Purchased	Tag Gen.	Price Paid	Value
218.				
219.				
220.				
221.				

Totals

222

Tuffy™
10" • Terrier • #4108 • Born: 10/12/96
Issued: 5/97 • Retired: 12/98
Market Value: ⑤–**$11** ④–**$13**

223

A.

B.

Tusk™
8" • Walrus • #4076 • Born: 9/18/95
Issued: Est. 6/95 • Retired: 1/97
Market Value:
A. "Tusk™" Swing Tag (6/95-1/97)
④–**$115** ③–**$180**
B. "Tuck™" Swing Tag (Est. Early 96-1/97) ④–**$130**

224

Twigs™
9" • Giraffe • #4068 • Born: 5/19/95
Issued: 1/96 • Retired: 5/98
Market Value: ⑤–**$20** ④–**$22** ③–**$90**

225

Ty 2K™
10" • Bear • #4262 • Born: 1/1/00
Issued: 8/99 • Retired: 12/99
Market Value: ⑤–**$32**

226

Valentina™
10" • Bear • #4233 • Born: 2/14/98
Issued: 1/99 • Retired: 12/99
Market Value: ⑤–**$14**

Beanie Babies®

	Date Purchased	Tag. Gen.	Price Paid	Value
222.				
223.				
224.				
225.				
226.				

Totals

Beanie Babies®

227

Valentino™
10" • Bear • #4058 • Born: 2/14/94
Issued: 1/95 • Retired: 12/98
Market Value: ⑤–**$22** ④–**$26**
③–**$145** ②–**$300**

228

Velvet™
10" • Panther • #4064 • Born: 12/16/95
Issued: 6/95 • Retired: 10/97
Market Value: ④–**$30** ③–**$95**

229

Waddle™
10" • Penguin • #4075 • Born: 12/19/95
Issued: 6/95 • Retired: 5/98
Market Value: ⑤–**$21** ④–**$23** ③–**$90**

230

Wallace™
10" • Bear • #4264 • Born: 1/25/99
Issued: 8/99 • Retired: 12/99
Market Value: ⑤–**$33**

231

Waves™
10" • Whale • #4084 • Born: 12/8/96
Issued: 5/97 • Retired: 5/98
Market Value: ⑤–**$15** ④–**$18**

Beanie Babies®

	Date Purchased	Tag Gen.	Price Paid	Value
227.				
228.				
229.				
230.				
231.				

Totals

114

232

Web™
10" • Spider • #4041 • Born: N/A
Issued: 6/94 • Retired: 1/96
Market Value: ③–**$1,100**
②–**$1,200** ①–**$1,450**

233

Weenie™
9" • Dachshund • #4013 • Born: 7/20/95
Issued: 1/96 • Retired: 5/98
Market Value: ⑤–**$27**
④–**$29** ③–**$100**

234

Whisper™
8" • Deer • #4194 • Born: 4/5/97
Issued: 5/98 • Retired: 12/99
Market Value: ⑤–**$8**

235

New!

Wiggly™
9" • Octopus • #4275 • Born: 1/25/00
Issued: 2/00 • Current
Market Value: ⑥–**$_____**

236

Wise™
9" • Owl • #4187 • Born: 5/31/97
Issued: 5/98 • Retired: 12/98
Market Value: ⑤–**$24**

Beanie Babies®

	Date Purchased	Tag Gen.	Price Paid	Value
232.				
233.				
234.				
235.				
236.				
Totals				

237

Wiser™
9" • Owl • #4238 • Born: 6/4/99
Issued: 4/99 • Retired: 3/99
Market Value: ⑤–**$22**

238

Wrinkles™
10" • Bulldog • #4103 • Born: 5/1/96
Issued: 6/96 • Retired: 9/98
Market Value: ⑤–**$12** ④–**$14**

239

Zero™
6" • Penguin • #4207 • Born: 1/2/98
Issued: 9/98 • Retired: 12/98
Market Value: ⑤–**$25**

240

Ziggy™
10" • Zebra • #4063 • Born: 12/24/95
Issued: 6/95 • Retired: 5/98
Market Value: ⑤–**$19** ④–**$21** ③–**$90**

241 A.

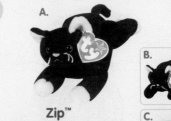

B.

C.

Zip™
10" • Cat • #4004 • Born: 3/28/94
Issued: 1/95 • Retired: 5/98
Market Value:
A. White Paws (3/96-5/98)
⑤–**$30** ④–**$33** ③–**$330**
B. All Black (1/96-3/96)
③–**$1,100**
C. White Face (1/95-1/96)
③–**$460** ②–**$540**

Beanie Babies®

	Date Purchased	Tag Gen.	Price Paid	Value
237.				
238.				
239.				
240.				
241.				

Totals

Sports Promotions

Since 1997, *Beanie Babies* have brought joy into the lives of sports fans everywhere as part of promotional giveaways for the NBA, WNBA, NHL, NFL and MLB, as well as the Canadian Special Olympics. To date, there have been 95 different promotions. "Chocolate" and "Curly" are the most popular giveaways, with five promotions apiece.

SPORTS PROMOTIONS® KEY

Canadian Special Olympics
National Football League
Major League Baseball
National Hockey League
National Basketball Association
Women's National Basketball Association

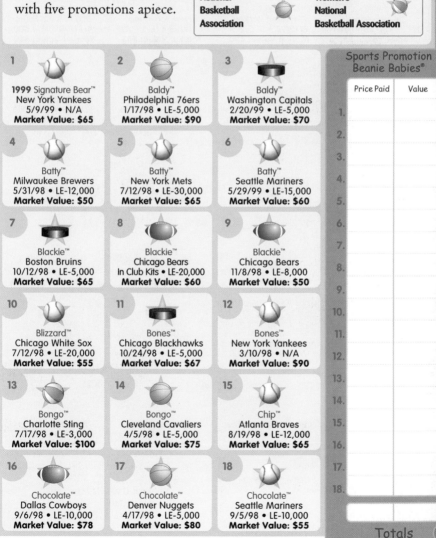

1 1999 Signature Bear™
New York Yankees
5/9/99 • N/A
Market Value: $65

2 Baldy™
Philadelphia 76ers
1/17/98 • LE-5,000
Market Value: $90

3 Baldy™
Washington Capitals
2/20/99 • LE-5,000
Market Value: $70

4 Batty™
Milwaukee Brewers
5/31/98 • LE-12,000
Market Value: $50

5 Batty™
New York Mets
7/12/98 • LE-30,000
Market Value: $65

6 Batty™
Seattle Mariners
5/29/99 • LE-15,000
Market Value: $60

7 Blackie™
Boston Bruins
10/12/98 • LE-5,000
Market Value: $65

8 Blackie™
Chicago Bears
In Club Kits • LE-20,000
Market Value: $60

9 Blackie™
Chicago Bears
11/8/98 • LE-8,000
Market Value: $50

10 Blizzard™
Chicago White Sox
7/12/98 • LE-20,000
Market Value: $55

11 Bones™
Chicago Blackhawks
10/24/98 • LE-5,000
Market Value: $67

12 Bones™
New York Yankees
3/10/98 • N/A
Market Value: $90

13 Bongo™
Charlotte Sting
7/17/98 • LE-3,000
Market Value: $100

14 Bongo™
Cleveland Cavaliers
4/5/98 • LE-5,000
Market Value: $75

15 Chip™
Atlanta Braves
8/19/98 • LE-12,000
Market Value: $65

16 Chocolate™
Dallas Cowboys
9/6/98 • LE-10,000
Market Value: $78

17 Chocolate™
Denver Nuggets
4/17/98 • LE-5,000
Market Value: $80

18 Chocolate™
Seattle Mariners
9/5/98 • LE-10,000
Market Value: $55

Sports Promotion Beanie Babies®

	Price Paid	Value
1.		
2.		
3.		
4.		
5.		
6.		
7.		
8.		
9.		
10.		
11.		
12.		
13.		
14.		
15.		
16.		
17.		
18.		

Totals

Value Guide — Ty® Plush Animals

19
Chocolate™
Tennessee Oilers
10/18/98 • LE-7,500
Market Value: $57

20
Chocolate™
Toronto Maple Leafs
1/2/99 • LE-3,000
Market Value: $100

21
Claude™
Sacramento Kings
3/14/99 • LE-5,000
Market Value: $125

22
Cubbie™
Chicago Cubs
1/15-1/17/99 • N/A
Market Value: $350

23
Cubbie™
Chicago Cubs
1/16-1/18/98 • LE-100
Market Value: $385

24
Cubbie™
Chicago Cubs
5/18/97 • LE-10,000
Market Value: $125

25
Cubbie™
Chicago Cubs
9/6/97 • LE-10,000
Market Value: $100

26
Curly™
Charlotte Sting
6/15/98 • LE-5,000
Market Value: $95

27
Curly™
Chicago Bears
12/20/98 • LE-10,000
Market Value: $55

28
Curly™
Cleveland Rockers
8/15/98 • LE-3,200
Market Value: $80

29
Curly™
New York Mets
8/22/98 • LE-30,000
Market Value: $65

30
Curly™
San Antonio Spurs
4/27/98 • LE-2,500
Market Value: $80

31
Daisy™
Chicago Cubs
5/3/98 • LE-10,000
Market Value: $250

32
Derby™
Houston Astros
8/16/98 • LE-15,000
Market Value: $65

33
Derby™
Indianapolis Colts
10/4/98 • LE-10,000
Market Value: $60

34
Dotty™
Los Angeles Sparks
7/31/98 • LE-3,000
Market Value: $70

35
Early™
Milwaukee Brewers
6/12/99 • LE-12,000
Market Value: $40

36
Ears™
Oakland A's
3/15/98 • LE-1,500
Market Value: $90

37
Erin™
Chicago Cubs
8/5/99 • LE-12,000
Market Value: $60

38
Fortune™
Kansas City Royals
6/6/99 • LE-10,000
Market Value: $55

39
Glory™
All-Star Game
7/7/98 • LE-52,000 approx.
Market Value: $150

40
Goatee™
Arizona Diamondbacks
7/8/99 • LE-10,000
Market Value: $50

41
Gobbles™
Phoenix Coyotes
11/26/98 • LE-5,000
Market Value: $60

42
Gobbles™
St. Louis Blues
11/24/98 • LE-7,500
Market Value: $60

43
Goochy™
Tampa Bay Devil Rays
4/10/99 • LE-10,000
Market Value: $52

44
Gracie™
Chicago Cubs
9/13/98 • LE-10,000
Market Value: $85

45
Hippie™
Minnesota Twins
6/18/99 • LE-10,000
Market Value: $55

46
Hippie™
St. Louis Blues
3/22/99 • LE-7,500
Market Value: $75

Value Guide — Ty® Plush Animals

47
Hissy™
Arizona Diamondbacks
6/14/98 • LE-6,500
Market Value: $60

48
KuKu™
Detroit Tigers
7/11/99 • LE-10,000
Market Value: $50

49
Lucky™
Minnesota Twins
7/31/98 • LE-10,000
Market Value: $55

50
Luke™
Texas Rangers
9/5/99 • LE-15,000
Market Value: $60

51
Mac™
St. Louis Cardinals
6/14/99 • LE-20,000
Market Value: $55

52
Maple™
Canadian Special Olympics
8/97 & 12/97 • N/A
Market Value: $350

53
Mel™
Anaheim Angels
9/6/98 • LE-10,000
Market Value: $60

54
Mel™
Detroit Shock
7/25/98 • LE-5,000
Market Value: $65

55
Millennium™
Chicago Cubs
9/26/99 • LE-40,000
Market Value: $70

56
Millennium™
New York Yankees
8/15/99 • N/A
Market Value: $70

57
Mystic™
Los Angeles Sparks
8/3/98 • LE-5,000
Market Value: $60

58
Mystic™
Washington Mystics
7/11/98 • LE-5,000
Market Value: $85

59
Peace™
Oakland A's
5/1/99 • LE-10,000
Market Value: $65

60
Peanut™
Oakland A's
8/1/98 • LE-15,000
Market Value: $55

61
Peanut™
Oakland A's
9/6/98 • LE-15,000
Market Value: $55

62
Pinky™
San Antonio Spurs
4/29/98 • LE-2,500
Market Value: $70

63
Pinky™
Tampa Bay Devil Rays
8/23/98 • LE-10,000
Market Value: $50

64
Pugsly™
Atlanta Braves
9/2/98 • LE-12,000
Market Value: $50

65
Pugsly™
Texas Rangers
8/4/98 • LE-10,000
Market Value: $52

66
Roam™
Buffalo Sabres
2/19/99 • LE-5,000
Market Value: $55

67
Roary™
Kansas City Royals
5/31/98 • LE-13,000
Market Value: $55

68
Rocket™
Toronto Blue Jays
9/6/98 • LE-12,000
Market Value: $55

69
Rover™
Cincinnati Reds
8/16/98 • LE-15,000
Market Value: $55

70
Sammy™
Chicago Cubs
1/15-1/17/99 • N/A
Market Value: $425

71
Sammy™
Chicago Cubs
4/25/99 • LE-12,000
Market Value: $70

72
Scoop™
Houston Comets
8/6/98 • LE-5,000
Market Value: $80

73
Scorch™
Cincinnati Reds
6/19/99 • LE-10,000
Market Value: $50

74
Slippery™
San Francisco Giants
4/11/99 • LE-15,000
Market Value: $50

Value Guide — Ty® Plush Animals

75
Sly™
Arizona Diamondbacks
8/27/98 • LE-10,000
Market Value: $60

76
Smoochy™
St. Louis Cardinals
8/14/98 • LE-20,000
Market Value: $54

77
Snort™
Chicago Bulls
4/10/99 • LE-5,000
Market Value: $60

78
Spunky™
Buffalo Sabres
10/23/98 • LE-5,000
Market Value: $50

79
Stretch™
New York Yankees
8/9/98 • N/A
Market Value: $55

80
Stretch™
St. Louis Cardinals
5/22/98 • LE-20,000
Market Value: $55

81
Stripes™
Detroit Tigers
5/31/98 • LE-10,000
Market Value: $60

82
Stripes™
Detroit Tigers
8/8/98 • LE-10,000
Market Value: $50

83
Strut™
Indiana Pacers
4/2/98 • LE-5,000
Market Value: $70

84
Tiny™
Houston Astros
7/18/99 • LE-20,000
Market Value: $95

85
Tuffy™
New Jersey Devils
10/24/98 • LE-5,000
Market Value: $65

86
Tuffy™
San Francisco Giants
8/30/98 • LE-10,000
Market Value: $55

87
Valentina™
New York Mets
5/30/99 • LE-18,000
Market Value: $60

88
Valentino™
Canadian Special Olympics
6/98, 9/98 & 10/98 • N/A
Market Value: $135

89
Valentino™
New York Yankees
5/17/98 • LE-10,000
Market Value: $135

90
Waddle™
Pittsburgh Penguins
10/24/98 • LE-7,000
Market Value: $60

91
Waddle™
Pittsburgh Penguins
11/21/98 • LE-7,000
Market Value: $60

92
Waves™
San Diego Padres
8/14/98 • LE-10,000
Market Value: $55

93
Weenie™
Tampa Bay Devil Rays
7/26/98 • LE-15,000
Market Value: $60

94
Whisper™
Milwaukee Bucks
2/28/99 • LE-5,000
Market Value: $50

Beanie Buddies are starting to make their mark as promotional giveaways at sporting events, too.

95
Peace™
Chicago Cubs
4/30/00 • LE-12,000
Market Value: N/E

Sports Promotion Beanie Babies®		
	Price Paid	Value
75.		
76.		
77.		
78.		
79.		
80.		
81.		
82.		
83.		
84.		
85.		
86.		
87.		
88.		
89.		
90.		
91.		
92.		
93.		
94.		
Sports Promotion Beanie Buddies®		
95.		

Totals

Beanie Buddies®

Since the original nine *Beanie Buddies* pieces made their debut in 1998, this collection has rapidly expanded to 76 animals! Included among the exciting 2000 releases are several who seem to have had quite a growth spurt or two! One such *Buddy* is "Jumbo Peace," who is larger than a small child (and probably weighs more, too!).

The 2000 *Beanie Buddies* also have a new swing tag, which means the secondary market value for *Beanie Buddies* is now based on tag generation.

TAG KEY

2 – 2nd Generation

1 – 1st Generation

1.

New!

2000 Signature Bear™
16" • Bear • #9348
Issued: 1/00 • Current
Market Value: 2 – $____

2.

Amber™
13" • Cat • #9341
Issued: 8/99 • Current
Market Value: 2 – $____   1 – $20

3.

Beak™
12" • Kiwi • #9301
Issued: 9/98 • Retired: 3/99
Market Value: 1 – $47

Beanie Buddies®

	Date Purchased	Tag Gen.	Price Paid	Value
1.				
2.				
3.				

Totals

121

Beanie Buddies®

4

Bongo™
13" • Monkey • #9312
Issued: 1/99 • Retired: 12/99
Market Value: ❶– **$18**

5

Britannia™
(exclusive to the United Kingdom)
16" • Bear • #9601
Issued: 8/99 • Current
Market Value: ❷–$_____ ❶– **$150**

6

New!

Bronty™
16" • Brontosaurus • #9353
Issued: 1/00 • Current
Market Value: ❷–$_____

7

Bubbles™
13" • Fish • #9323
Issued: 1/99 • Retired: 11/99
Market Value: ❶– **$23**

Beanie Buddies®

	Date Purchased	Tag Gen.	Price Paid	Value
4.				
5.				
6.				
7.				
8.				

Totals

8

Chilly™
16" • Polar Bear • #9317
Issued: 1/99 • Retired: 11/99
Market Value: ❶– **$22**

Value Guide — Ty® Plush Animals

9

Chip™
16" • Cat • #9318
Issued: 1/99 • Retired: 12/99
Market Value: ❶ – **$23**

10

New!

Chocolate™
16" • Moose • #9349
Issued: 1/00 • Current
Market Value: ❷ – $____

11

Clubby™
16" • Bear • #9990
Issued: 8/99 • Current
Market Value: ❶ – $____

12

Clubby II™
16" • Bear • #9991
Issued: 8/99 • Current
Market Value: ❶ – $____

13

New!

Congo™
16" • Gorilla • #9361
Issued: 1/00 • Current
Market Value: ❷ – $____

Beanie Buddies®

	Date Purchased	Tag Gen.	Price Paid	Value
9.				
10.				
11.				
12.				
13.				

Totals

14

New!

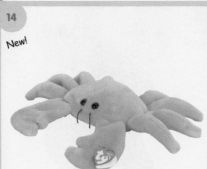

Digger™
13" • Crab • #9351
Issued: 1/00 • Current
Market Value: ②–$_____

15

New!

Dotty™
13" • Dalmatian • #9364
Issued: 1/00 • Current
Market Value: ②–$_____

16

New!

Dragon™
16" • Dragon • #9365
Issued: 1/00 • Current
Market Value: ②–$_____

17

New!

Erin™
16" • Bear • #9309
Issued: 1/99 • Retired: 11/99
Market Value: ①–$36

Beanie Buddies®

	Date Purchased	Tag Gen.	Price Paid	Value
14.				
15.				
16.				
17.				
18.				

Totals

18

Eucalyptus™
16" • Koala • #9363
Issued: 1/00 • Current
Market Value: ②–$_____

Value Guide — Ty® Plush Animals

19
New!

Extra Large Hippie™
27" • Bunny • #9038
Issued: 1/00 • Current
Market Value: ②–$_____

20
New!

Extra Large Peace™
27" • Bear • #9036
Issued: 1/00 • Current
Market Value: ②–$_____

21

Fetch™
13" • Golden Retriever • #9338
Issued: 8/99 • Retired 3/00
Market Value: ②–N/E ①–$24

22
New!

Flip™
13" • Cat • #9359
Issued: 1/00 • Current
Market Value: ②–$_____

23
New!

Flippity™
16" • Bunny • #9358
Issued: 1/00 • Current
Market Value: ②–$_____

Beanie Buddies®

	Date Purchased	Tag Gen.	Price Paid	Value
19.				
20.				
21.				
22.				
23.				

Totals

24

Fuzz™
16" • Bear • #9328
Issued: 4/99 • Current
Market Value: ②–$_____ ①–**$27**

25

Gobbles™
13" • Turkey • #9333
Issued: 8/99 • Retired: 12/99
Market Value: ①–**$24**

26

New!

Goochy™
13" • Jellyfish • #9362
Issued: 1/00 • Current
Market Value: ②–$_____

27

New!

Groovy™
16" • Bear • #9345
Issued: 1/00 • Current
Market Value: ②–$_____

Beanie Buddies®

	Date Purchased	Tag Gen.	Price Paid	Value
24.				
25.				
26.				
27.				
28.				

Totals

28

Halo™
16" • Angel Bear • #9337
Issued: 8/99 • Current
Market Value: ②–$_____ ①–**$40**

29

New!

Hippie™
16" • Bunny • #9357
Issued: 1/00 • Current
Market Value: ②–$_____

30

Hippity™
12" • Bunny • #9324
Issued: 1/99 • Retired: 12/99
Market Value: ①–$25

31

Hope™
13" • Bear • #9327
Issued: 4/99 • Current
Market Value: ②–$_____ ①–$23

32

Humphrey™
13" • Camel • #9307
Issued: 9/98 • Retired: 12/99
Market Value: ①–$33

33

Inch™
17" • Inchworm • #9331
Issued: Summer 1999 • Retired: 1/00
Market Value: ①–$20

Beanie Buddies®

	Date Purchased	Tag Gen.	Price Paid	Value
29.				
30.				
31.				
32.				
33.				

Totals

34

Jabber™
12" • Parrot • #9326
Issued: 4/99 • Retired: 12/99
Market Value: ①–**$20**

35

Jake™
12" • Mallard Duck • #9304
Issued: 9/98 • Retired: 12/99
Market Value: ①–**$27**

36

New!

Jumbo Peace™
48" • Bear • #9035
Issued: 1/00 • Current
Market Value: ②–**$_____**

37

New!

Kicks™
16" • Bear • #9343
Issued: 1/00 • Current
Market Value: ②–**$_____**

Beanie Buddies®

	Date Purchased	Tag Gen.	Price Paid	Value
34.				
35.				
36.				
37.				
38.				

Totals

38

New!

Large Fuzz™
22" • Bear • #9040
Issued: 1/00 • Current
Market Value: ②–**$_____**

39

New!

Large Hippie™
22" • Bunny • #9039
Issued: 1/00 • Current
Market Value: ②–$_____

40

New!

Large Peace™
22" • Bear • #9037
Issued: 1/00 • Current
Market Value: ②–$_____

41

New!

Lips™
13" • Fish • #9355
Issued: 1/00 • Current
Market Value: ②–$_____

42

New!

Lizzy™
16" • Lizard • #9366
Issued: 1/00 • Current
Market Value: ②–$_____

43

New!

Lucky™
13" • Ladybug • #9354
Issued: 1/00 • Current
Market Value: ②–$_____

Beanie Buddies®

	Date Purchased	Tag Gen.	Price Paid	Value
39.				
40.				
41.				
42.				
43.				
Totals				

Beanie Buddies®

44

Maple™
(exclusive to Canada)
16" • Bear • #9600
Issued: 8/99 • Current
Market Value: ❷–$_____ ❶–$135

45

Millennium™
16" • Bear • #9325
Issued: 4/99 • Retired: 11/99
Market Value: ❶–$34

46

New!

Nanook™
13" • Husky • #9350
Issued: 1/00 • Current
Market Value: ❷–$_____

47

New!

Osito™
(exclusive to the United States)
16" • Bear • #9344
Issued: 1/00 • Current
Market Value: ❷–$_____

Beanie Buddies®

	Date Purchased	Tag Gen.	Price Paid	Value
44.				
45.				
46.				
47.				
48.				

Totals

48

Patti™
13" • Platypus • #9320
Issued: 1/99 • Retired: 7/99
Market Value: ❶–$22

49

Peace™
16" • Bear • #9335
Issued: 8/99 • Current
Market Value: ②–$_____ ①–**$36**

50

B.

A.

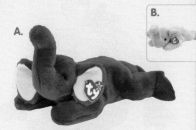

Peanut™
16" • Elephant • #9300
Issued: 9/98 • Retired: 2/00
Market Value:
A. Dark Blue ①–**$25** ②–**$25**
B. Light Blue ②–**$50**

51

Peking™
16" • Panda • #9310
Issued: 1/99 • Retired: 12/99
Market Value: ①–**$26**

52

Pinky™
16" • Flamingo • #9316
Issued: 1/99 • Retired: 12/99
Market Value: ①–**$18**

53

Princess™
16" • Bear • #9329
Issued: 4/99 • Current
Market Value: ②–$_____ ①–**$42**

Beanie Buddies®

	Date Purchased	Tag Gen.	Price Paid	Value
49.				
50.				
51.				
52.				
53.				

Totals

Beanie Buddies®

54

Pumkin'™
13" • Pumpkin • #9332
Issued: 8/99 • Retired: 11/99
Market Value: ①– **$27**

55

A.

B.

Quackers™
12" • Duck • #9302
Issued: 9/98 • Retired: 7/99
Market Value:
A. With Wings ①– **$30**
B. Without Wings ①– **$250**

56

New!

Rainbow™
16" • Chameleon • #9367
Issued: 1/00 • Current
Market Value: ②–$_____

57

Rover™
13" • Dog • #9305
Issued: 9/98 • Retired: 12/99
Market Value: ①– **$33**

58

Schweetheart™
12" • Orangutan • #9330
Issued: Summer 1999 • Retired: 1/00
Market Value: ①– **$20**

Beanie Buddies®

	Date Purchased	Tag Gen.	Price Paid	Value
54.				
55.				
56.				
57.				
58.				

Totals

59

Silver™
13" • Cat • #9340
Issued: 8/99 • Current
Market Value: ❷–$_____ ❶–**$23**

60

Slither™
16" • Snake • #9339
Issued: 8/99 • Current
Market Value: ❷–$_____ ❶–**$21**

61

Smoochy™
13" • Frog • #9315
Issued: 1/99 • Retired: 11/99
Market Value: ❶–**$24**

62

Snort™
16" • Bull • #9311
Issued: 1/99 • Retired: 12/99
Market Value: ❶–**$18**

63

Snowboy™
16" • Snowboy • #9342
Issued: 8/99 • Retired: 12/99
Market Value: ❶–**$30**

Beanie Buddies®

	Date Purchased	Tag Gen.	Price Paid	Value
59.				
60.				
61.				
62.				
63.				
Totals				

Beanie Buddies®

64

Spangle™
16" • Bear • #9336
Issued: 8/99 • Current
Market Value: ❷–$_____ ❶– $40

65

New!

Speedy™
13" • Turtle • #9352
Issued: 1/00 • Current
Market Value: ❷–$_____

66

Spinner™
13" • Spider • #9334
Issued: 8/99 • Retired: 12/99
Market Value: ❶– $20

67

Squealer™
16" • Pig • #9313
Issued: 1/99 • Retired: 11/99
Market Value: ❶– $20

Beanie Buddies®

	Date Purchased	Tag Gen.	Price Paid	Value
64.				
65.				
66.				
67.				
68.				

Totals

68

Stretch™
16" • Ostrich • #9303
Issued: 9/98 • Retired: 12/99
Market Value: ❶– $26

Value Guide — Ty® Plush Animals

69

Teddy™
16" • Bear • #9306
Issued: 9/98 • Retired: 11/99
Market Value: ❶– $40

70

Tracker™
13" • Basset Hound • #9319
Issued: 1/99 • Retired: 11/99
Market Value: ❶– $21

71

Twigs™
13" • Giraffe • #9308
Issued: 9/98 • Retired: 1/99
Market Value: ❶– $215

72

New!

Ty 2K™
16" • Bear • #9346
Issued: 1/00 • Retired: 3/00
Market Value: ❷– N/E

73

New!

Valentino™
16" • Bear • #9347
Issued: 1/00 • Current
Market Value: ❷– $_____

Beanie Buddies®

	Date Purchased	Tag Gen.	Price Paid	Value
69.				
70.				
71.				
72.				
73.				

Totals

74

Waddle™
12" • Penguin • #9314
Issued: 1/99 • Retired: 12/99
Market Value: ❶ – **$20**

75

New!

Weenie™
16" • Dachshund • #9356
Issued: 1/00 • Current
Market Value: ❷ – **$_____**

76

New!

Zip™
13" • Cat • #9360
Issued: 1/00 • Current
Market Value: ❷ – **$_____**

Beanie Buddies®

	Date Purchased	Tag Gen.	Price Paid	Value
74.				
75.				
76.				

Totals

Teenie Beanie Babies™

Ever since the first *Teenie Beanie Babies* promotion was held at McDonald's in the spring of 1997, collectors have been clamoring for more. Ty and McDonald's responded by holding two subsequent promotions in the United States in 1998 and 1999, as well as overseas. Collectors were especially excited by the 1999 promotion, which allowed people to purchase *Teenie Beanie* versions of hard-to-find international *Beanie Babies* such as "Erin," "Brittania," "Glory" and "Maple."

1997 Teenie Beanie Babies™ Complete Set (set/10)
Issued: 4/97 • Retired: 5/97
Market Value: $160

1998 Teenie Beanie Babies™ Complete Set (set/12)
Issued: 5/98 • Retired: 6/98
Market Value: $55

1999 Teenie Beanie Babies™ Complete Set (set/12)
Issued: 5/99 • Retired: 6/99
Market Value: $40

1999 Teenie Beanie Babies™ International Bears (set/4)
Issued: 6/99 • Retired: 6/99
Market Value: $30

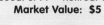

Antsy™
7" • Anteater
3rd Promotion, #2 of 12
Issued: 5/99 • Retired: 6/99
Market Value: $5

Bones™
6" • Dog
2nd Promotion, #9 of 12
Issued: 5/98 • Retired: 6/98
Market Value: $7

Bongo™
5" • Monkey
2nd Promotion, #2 of 12
Issued: 5/98 • Retired: 6/98
Market Value: $14

Teenie Beanie Babies™		
Date Purchased	Price Paid	Value
1.		
2.		
3.		
4.		
5.		
6.		
7.		
Totals		

Teenie Beanie Babies™

8

Britannia™
5" • Bear
4th Promotion
Issued: 6/99 • Retired: 6/99
Market Value: $10

9

Chip™
6.5" • Cat
3rd Promotion, #12 of 12
Issued: 5/99 • Retired: 6/99
Market Value: $5

10

Chocolate™
5.5" • Moose
1st Promotion, #4 of 10
Issued: 4/97 • Retired: 5/97
Market Value: $24

11

Chops™
5" • Lamb
1st Promotion, #3 of 10
Issued: 4/97 • Retired: 5/97
Market Value: $28

12

Claude™
5.5" • Crab
3rd Promotion, #9 of 12
Issued: 5/99 • Retired: 6/99
Market Value: $5

13

Doby™
4.5" • Doberman
2nd Promotion, #1 of 12
Issued: 5/98 • Retired: 6/98
Market Value: $12

14

Erin™
5" • Bear
4th Promotion
Issued: 6/99 • Retired: 6/99
Market Value: $10

15

Freckles™
6.5" • Leopard
3rd Promotion, #1 of 12
Issued: 5/99 • Retired: 6/99
Market Value: $5

16

A.

B.

Glory™
5" • Bear
4th Promotion
Issued: 6/99 • Retired: 6/99
Market Value:
A. Glory – **$10**
B. McDonald's Employee
Bear – **$24**

17

Goldie™
4.5" • Goldfish
1st Promotion, #5 of 10
Issued: 4/97 • Retired: 5/97
Market Value: $20

Teenie Beanie Babies™

	Date Purchased	Price Paid	Value
8.			
9.			
10.			
11.			
12.			
13.			
14.			
15.			
16.			
17.			
Totals			

18

Happy™
6" • Hippo
2nd Promotion, #6 of 12
Issued: 5/98 • Retired: 6/98
Market Value: $6

19

Iggy™
7" • Iguana
3rd Promotion, #6 of 12
Issued: 5/99 • Retired: 6/99
Market Value: $5

20

Inch™
7.5" • Inchworm
2nd Promotion, #4 of 12
Issued: 5/98 • Retired: 6/98
Market Value: $6

21

Lizz™
8" • Lizard
1st Promotion, #10 of 10
Issued: 4/97 • Retired: 5/97
Market Value: $15

22

Maple™
5" • Bear
4th Promotion
Issued: 6/99 • Retired: 6/99
Market Value: $10

23

Mel™
5" • Koala
2nd Promotion, #7 of 12
Issued: 5/98 • Retired: 6/98
Market Value: $6

24

¯Nook™
5.5" • Husky
3rd Promotion, #11 of 12
Issued: 5/99 • Retired: 6/99
Market Value: $5

25

Nuts™
4" • Squirrel
3rd Promotion, #8 of 12
Issued: 5/99 • Retired: 6/99
Market Value: $5

26

Patti™
5.5" • Platypus
1st Promotion, #1 of 10
Issued: 4/97 • Retired: 5/97
Market Value: $30

27

Peanut™
6" • Elephant
2nd Promotion, #12 of 12
Issued: 5/98 • Retired: 6/98
Market Value: $7

	Teenie Beanie Babies™		
	Date Purchased	Price Paid	Value
18.			
19.			
20.			
21.			
22.			
23.			
24.			
25.			
26.			
27.			
	Totals		

28

Pinchers™
6.5" • Lobster
2nd Promotion, #5 of 12
Issued: 5/98 • Retired: 6/98
Market Value: $6

29

Pinky™
7" • Flamingo
1st Promotion, #2 of 10
Issued: 4/97 • Retired: 5/97
Market Value: $36

30

Quacks™
3.5" • Duck
1st Promotion, #9 of 10
Issued: 4/97 • Retired: 5/97
Market Value: $16

31

Rocket™
6" • Blue Jay
3rd Promotion, #5 of 12
Issued: 5/99 • Retired: 6/99
Market Value: $5

32

Scoop™
4" • Pelican
2nd Promotion, #8 of 12
Issued: 5/98 • Retired: 6/98
Market Value: $7

33

Seamore™
4.5" • Seal
1st Promotion, #7 of 10
Issued: 4/97 • Retired: 5/97
Market Value: $24

34

Smoochy™
5" • Frog
3rd Promotion, #3 of 12
Issued: 5/99 • Retired: 6/99
Market Value: $5

35

Snort™
6" • Bull
1st Promotion, #8 of 10
Issued: 4/97 • Retired: 5/97
Market Value: $17

36

Speedy™
4" • Turtle
1st Promotion, #6 of 10
Issued: 4/97 • Retired: 5/97
Market Value: $20

37

Spunky™
5.5" • Cocker Spaniel
3rd Promotion, #4 of 12
Issued: 5/99 • Retired: 6/99
Market Value: $5

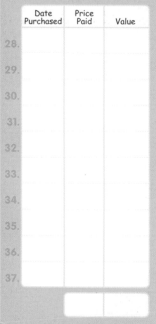

Teenie Beanie Babies™

	Date Purchased	Price Paid	Value
28.			
29.			
30.			
31.			
32.			
33.			
34.			
35.			
36.			
37.			

Totals

38

Stretchy™
7" • Ostrich
3rd Promotion, #10 of 12
Issued: 5/99 • Retired: 6/99
Market Value: $5

39

Strut™
6" • Rooster
3rd Promotion, #7 of 12
Issued: 5/99 • Retired: 6/99
Market Value: $5

40

Twigs™
6" • Giraffe
2nd Promotion, #3 of 12
Issued: 5/98 • Retired: 6/98
Market Value: $12

41

Waddle™
5" • Penguin
2nd Promotion, #11 of 12
Issued: 5/98 • Retired: 6/98
Market Value: $7

42

Zip™
5" • Cat
2nd Promotion, #10 of 12
Issued: 5/98 • Retired: 6/98
Market Value: $8

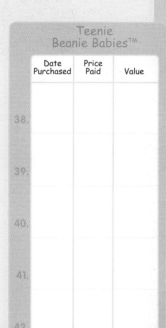

| Teenie Beanie Babies™ | | |
Date Purchased	Price Paid	Value
38.		
39.		
40.		
41.		
42.		
Totals		

Beanie Kids™

Unexpected news from Ty, Inc. was the introduction of a new line, called *Beanie Kids,* which tumbled onto the Ty plush scene in January, 2000. The *Beanie Kids* are nine adorable boys and girls who are ready to bring a "human" element to *Beanie Babies* collecting.

Each *Beanie Kid's* swing tag opens to reveal his or her name, birthdate and a short poem. These tykes have been enthusiastically embraced by *Beanie Babies* collectors of all ages, and although the collection is small now, the *Beanie Kids* line is sure to grow as fast as kids themselves.

1

New!

Angel™
10" • #0001 • Born: 3/29/94
Issued: 1/00 • Current
Market Value: $_____

2

New!

Boomer™
10" • #0007 • Born: 8/11/94
Issued: 1/00 • Current
Market Value: $_____

3

New!

Chipper™
10" • #0008 • Born: 7/20/97
Issued: 1/00 • Current
Market Value: $_____

Beanie Kids™

	Date Purchased	Price Paid	Value
1.			
2.			
3.			

Totals

4

New!

Curly™
10" • #0004 • Born: 3/2/97
Issued: 1/00 • Current
Market Value: $_____

5

New!

Cutie™
10" • #0005 • Born: 12/26/96
Issued: 1/00 • Current
Market Value: $_____

6

New!

Ginger™
10" • #0003 • Born: 6/12/92
Issued: 1/00 • Current
Market Value: $_____

7

New!

Precious™
10" • #0002 • Born: 5/15/93
Issued: 1/00 • Current
Market Value: $_____

Beanie Kids™

	Date Purchased	Price Paid	Value
4.			
5.			
6.			
7.			

Totals

8

New!

Rascal™
10" • #0006 • Born: 4/15/95
Issued: 1/00 • Current
Market Value: $_____

9

New!

Tumbles™
10" • #0009 • Born: 9/3/96
Issued: 1/00 • Current
Market Value: $_____

Beanie Kids™

	Date Purchased	Price Paid	Value
8.			
9.			

Totals

Pillow Pals®

The 44 members of the *Pillow Pals* family have all bid "adieu" to life in the fast lane and have headed for retirement. Although no new *Pillow Pals* have been released since 1999, no official word on the fate of *The Pillow Pals Collection* has been announced, so the future of this collection is anyone's guess.

1

Antlers™
14" • Moose • #3028
Issued: 1998 • Retired: 1998
Market Value: $25

2

Antlers™
14" • Moose • #3104
Issued: 1999 • Retired: 1999
Market Value: $12

3

Ba Ba™
15" • Lamb • #3008
Issued: 1997 • Retired: 1998
Market Value: $17

4

Ba Ba™
15" • Lamb • #3113
Issued: 1999 • Retired: 1999
Market Value: $12

5

Bruiser™
14" • Bulldog • #3018
Issued: 1997 • Retired: 1998
Market Value: $12

Pillow Pals®

	Date Purchased	Price Paid	Value
1.			
2.			
3.			
4.			
5.			
Totals			

6

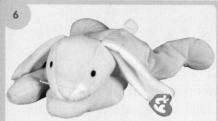

Carrots™
15" • Bunny • #3010
Issued: 1997 • Retired: 1998
Market Value: $15

7

Carrots™
15" • Bunny • #3101
Issued: 1999 • Retired: 1999
Market Value: $12

8

Chewy™
15" • Beaver • #3105
Issued: 1999 • Retired: 1999
Market Value: $12

9

Clover™
15" • Rabbit • #3020
Issued: 1998 • Retired: 1998
Market Value: $20

10

Foxy™
19" • Fox • #3022
Issued: 1998 • Retired: 1998
Market Value: $16

11

Glide™
14" • Porpoise • #3025
Issued: 1998 • Retired: 1998
Market Value: $14

Pillow Pals®

	Date Purchased	Price Paid	Value
6.			
7.			
8.			
9.			
10.			
11.			
Totals			

Value Guide — Ty® Plush Animals

12

Huggy™
14" • Bear • #3002
Issued: 1995 • Retired: 1998
A. Pink Ribbon (1997-98)
B. Blue Ribbon (1995-97)
Market Value: A/B—$27

13

Huggy™
15" • Bear • #3111
Issued: 1999 • Retired: 1999
Market Value: $12

14

Kolala™
15" • Koala • #3108
Issued: 1999 • Retired: 1999
Market Value: $12

15

Meow™
15" • Cat • #3011
Issued: 1997 • Retired: 1998
A. Tan (1997-98)
B. Gray (1997)
Market Value: A—$16 B—$140

16

Meow™
15" • Cat • #3107
Issued: 1999 • Retired: 1999
Market Value: $12

17

Moo™
16" • Cow • #3004
Issued: 1995 • Retired: 1998
Market Value: $18

18

Oink™
15" • Pig • #3005
Issued: 1995 • Retired: 1998
Market Value: $20

Pillow Pals®

	Date Purchased	Price Paid	Value
12.			
13.			
14.			
15.			
16.			
17.			
18.			
Totals			

19

Paddles™
15" • Platypus • #3026
Issued: 1998 • Retired: 1998
Market Value: $12

20

Paddles™
15" • Platypus • #3103
Issued: 1999 • Retired: 1999
Market Value: $12

21

Purr™
15" • Tiger • #3016
Issued: 1997 • Retired: 1998
Market Value: $21

22

Red™
15" • Bull • #3021
Issued: 1998 • Retired: 1998
Market Value: $18

23

Ribbit™
14" • Frog • #3006
Issued: 1995 • Retired: 1996
Market Value: $410

24

Ribbit™
14" • Frog • #3009
Issued: 1997 • Retired: 1998
Market Value: $17

25

Ribbit™
14" • Frog • #3106
Issued: 1999 • Retired: 1999
Market Value: $12

Pillow Pals®

	Date Purchased	Price Paid	Value
19.			
20.			
21.			
22.			
23.			
24.			
25.			
Totals			

26

Rusty™
15" • Raccoon • #3100
Issued: 1999 • Retired: 1999
Market Value: $12

27

Sherbet™
15" • Bear • #3027
Issued: 1998 • Retired: 1998
Market Value: $15

28

Sherbet™
15" • Bear • #3112
Issued: 1999 • Retired: 1999
Market Value: $12

29

Snap™
14" • Turtle • #3007
Issued: 1995 • Retired: 1996
Market Value: $365

30

Snap™
14" • Turtle • #3015
Issued: 1997 • Retired: 1998
Market Value: $23

31

Snap™
14" • Turtle • #3102
Issued: 1999 • Retired: 1999
Market Value: $12

32

Snuggy™
14" • Bear • #3001
Issued: 1995 • Retired: 1998
A. Blue Ribbon (1997-98)
B. Pink Ribbon (1995-97)
Market Value: A/B–$28

Pillow Pals®

	Date Purchased	Price Paid	Value
26.			
27.			
28.			
29.			
30.			
31.			
32.			
Totals			

Pillow Pals®

33

Sparkler™
14" • Bear • #3115
Issued: 1999 • Retired: 1999
Market Value: $14

34

Speckles™
15" • Leopard • #3017
Issued: 1997 • Retired: 1998
Market Value: $15

35

Spotty™
15" • Dalmatian • #3019
Issued: 1998 • Retired: 1998
Market Value: $15

36

Squirt™
15" • Elephant • #3013
Issued: 1997 • Retired: 1998
Market Value: $15

37

Squirt™
15" • Elephant • #3109
Issued: 1999 • Retired: 1999
Market Value: $12

38

Swinger™
15" • Monkey • #3023
Issued: 1998 • Retired: 1998
Market Value: $15

39

Pillow Pals®

	Date Purchased	Price Paid	Value
33.			
34.			
35.			
36.			
37.			
38.			
39.			

Totals

Swinger™
15" • Monkey • #3110
Issued: 1999 • Retired: 1999
Market Value: $12

Value Guide — Ty® Plush Animals

40

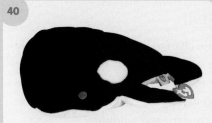

Tide™
14" • Whale • #3024
Issued: 1998 • Retired: 1998
Market Value: $13

41

Tubby™
15" • Hippo • #3012
Issued: 1997 • Retired: 1998
Market Value: $16

42

Woof™
15" • Dog • #3003
Issued: 1995 • Retired: 1998
Market Value: $16

43

Woof™
15" • Dog • #3114
Issued: 1999 • Retired: 1999
Market Value: $12

44

Zulu™
15" • Zebra • #3014
Issued: 1997 • Retired: 1998
A. Thick Stripes (1997-98)
B. Thin Stripes (1997)
Market Value: A/B–$20

Pillow Pals®

	Date Purchased	Price Paid	Value
40.			
41.			
42.			
43.			
44.			
Totals			

Ty Classic™

The new millennium heralded a name change for this line. Previously referred to as *Ty Plush*, the collection is now called *Ty Classic*. The line made its debut in 1986, making it the oldest in the Ty family. Today, the menagerie has grown so large that this value guide divides the collection into five groupings: bears, cats, dogs, country and wildlife.

Nineteen new pieces were introduced into the *Ty Classic* family this year, bringing the total number of pieces to 382.

Bears

Since the first bears were released in 1988, bears have become the most sizeable contingent of the *Ty Classic*™ family tree. In January of 2000, Ty introduced eight new bears, bringing the grand total to 140 pieces.

1991 Ty Collectable Bear™
21" • Bear • #5500
Issued: 1991 • Retired: 1991
Market Value: $1,250

1992 Ty Collectable Bear™
21" • Bear • #5500
Issued: 1992 • Retired: 1992
A. "1992 Ty Collectable Bear™" Version
B. "Edmond™" Version
Market Value: A–$580 B–$200

1997 Holiday Bear™
14" • Bear • #5700
Issued: 1997 • Retired: 1997
Market Value: $35

Bears

Date Purchased	Price Paid	Value
1.		
2.		
3.		
Totals		

4

Aurora™
13" • Polar Bear • #5103
Issued: 1996 • Retired: 1997
Market Value: $45

5

Baby Buddy™
20" • Bear • #5011
Issued: 1992 • Retired: 1992
Market Value: $425

6

Baby Cinnamon™
13" • Bear • #5105
Issued: 1996 • Retired: 1996
Market Value: $45

7

Baby Curly™
12" • Bear • #5017
Issued: 1993 • Retired: 1997
Market Value: $35

8

Baby Curly™
(moved from Attic Treasures™ in 2000)
12" • Bear • #5018 • Issued: 1993 • Current
A. Leaf Sweater, Ty Classic Swing Tag (2000-Current)
B. USA Sweater, Attic Treasures Swing Tag (1999-2000)
C. USA Sweater, Ty Plush Swing Tag (1998-99)
D. Ribbon, Ty Plush Swing Tag (1993-98)
Market Value: A– $_____ B– $40 C–$30 D–$20

9

Baby Ginger™
14" • Bear • #5108
Issued: 1997 • Retired: 1998
Market Value: $20

Bears

	Date Purchased	Price Paid	Value
4.			
5.			
6.			
7.			
8.			
9.			
Totals			

Ty Classic™

10

Baby Paws™
12" • Bear • #5110
Issued: 1997 • Current
Market Value: $_____

11

Baby Paws™
12" • Bear • #5111
Issued: 1997 • Current
Market Value: $_____

12

Baby Paws™
12" • Bear • #5112
Issued: 1998 • Retired: 1998
Market Value: $20

13

Baby PJ™
12" • Bear • #5016
Issued: 1993 • Retired: 1998
Market Value: $24

14

Baby PJ™
12" • Bear • #5100
Issued: 1994 • Retired: 1994
Market Value: $112

15

Baby Powder™
14" • Bear • #5109
Issued: 1997 • Retired: 1998
Market Value: $18

16

Baby Spice™
13" • Bear • #5104
Issued: 1996 • Retired: 1997
A. "Baby Spice™" Swing Tag
B. "ByBy Spice™" Swing Tag
Market Value: A/B–$35

Bears

	Date Purchased	Price Paid	Value
10.			
11.			
12.			
13.			
14.			
15.			
16.			
Totals			

17

Bailey™
19" • Bear • #5502
Issued: 1997 • Retired: 1997
Market Value: $50

18

New!

Bamboo™
17" • Panda • #5033
Issued: 2000 • Current
Market Value: $_____

19

Bamboo™
13" • Panda • #5106
Issued: 1996 • Retired: 1997
Market Value: $40

20

Bamboo™
12" • Panda • #5113
Issued: 1998 • Retired: 1998
Market Value: $15

21

Baron™
18" • Bear • #5200
Issued: 1995 • Retired: 1995
Market Value: $112

22

Beanie Bear™
12" • Bear • #5000
Issued: 1988 • Retired: 1990
Market Value: $815

23

Beanie Bear™
12" • Bear • #5100
Issued: 1991 • Retired: 1992
Market Value: $525

Bears

	Date Purchased	Price Paid	Value
17.			
18.			
19.			
20.			
21.			
22.			
23.			
Totals			

Ty Classic™

24

Beanie Bear™
12" • Bear • #5101
Issued: 1991 • Retired: 1991
Market Value: $1,000

25

Beanie Bear™
12" • Bear • #5102
Issued: 1991 • Retired: 1991
Market Value: $1,000

26

New!

Belvedere™
17" • Bear • #5031
Issued: 2000 • Current
Market Value: $____

27

Big Beanie Bear™
15" • Bear • #5011
Issued: 1990 • Retired: 1990
Market Value: $780

28

Big Beanie Bear™
15" • Bear • #5200
Issued: 1991 • Retired: 1991
Market Value: $650

29

Big Beanie Bear™
15" • Bear • #5201
Issued: 1991 • Retired: 1991
Market Value: $500

30

Big Beanie Bear™
15" • Bear • #5202
Issued: 1991 • Retired: 1991
Market Value: $700

Bears

	Date Purchased	Price Paid	Value
24.			
25.			
26.			
27.			
28.			
29.			
30.			
Totals			

31

Big Pudgy™
28" • Bear • #9006
Issued: 1994 • Retired: 1996
Market Value: $230

32

Big Shaggy™
26" • Bear • #9015
Issued: 1992 • Retired: 1992
Market Value: $460

33

Blackie™
13" • Bear • #5003
Issued: 1988 • Retired: 1990
Market Value: $500

34

Bluebeary™
14" • Bear • #5312
Issued: 1999 • Current
Market Value: $_____

35

New!

Broderick™
17" • Bear • #5032
Issued: 2000 • Current
Market Value: $_____

36

Brownie™
13" • Bear • #5100
Issued: 1996 • Retired: 1996
Market Value: $73

Bears

	Date Purchased	Price Paid	Value
31.			
32.			
33.			
34.			
35.			
36.			
Totals			

157

37

Buddy™
20" • Bear • #5007
Issued: 1990 • Retired: 1992
Market Value: $515

38

Buddy™
20" • Bear • #5019
Issued: 1993 • Retired: 1996
Market Value: $42

39

Butterbeary™
14" • Bear • #5311
Issued: 1999 • Current
Market Value: $_____

40

Cinnamon™
13" • Bear • #5004
Issued: 1989 • Retired: 1990
Market Value: $900

41

Cinnamon™
18" • Bear • #5021
Issued: 1996 • Retired: 1996
Market Value: $55

42

Cocoa™
12" • Bear • #5107
Issued: 1997 • Retired: 1998
Market Value: $15

43

Curly™
18" • Bear • #5300
Issued: 1991 • Retired: 1997
A. 18" (1993-97)
B. 22" (1991-92)
Market Value: A/B–$56

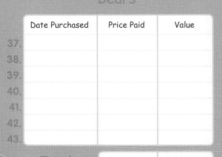

Bears

	Date Purchased	Price Paid	Value
37.			
38.			
39.			
40.			
41.			
42.			
43.			
Totals			

44

Curly™
22" • Bear • #5301
Issued: 1991 • Retired: 1991
Market Value: $400

45

Curly™
(moved from Attic Treasures™ in 2000)
18" • Bear • #5302 • Issued: 1991 • Current
A. 18", Umbrella Sweater, Ty Classic Swing Tag (2000-Current)
B. 18", Flag Sweater, Attic Treasures Swing Tag (1999-2000)
C. 18", Flag Sweater, Ty Plush Swing Tag (1998-99)
D. 18", Ribbon, Ty Plush Swing Tag (1993-98)
E. 22", Ty Plush Swing Tag (1991-92)
Market Value: A– $_____ B/C– **$30** D/E– **$25**

46

Cuzzy™
13" • Bear • #5203
Issued: 1996 • Retired: 1997
Market Value: $70

47

Dumpling™
12" • Bear • #5022
Issued: 1996 • Retired: 1996
Market Value: $65

48

Dumpling™
12" • Bear • #5023
Issued: 1996 • Retired: 1996
Market Value: $60

49

Eleanor™
19" • Bear • #5500
Issued: 1996 • Retired: 1997
Market Value: $85

50

Faith™
10" • Bear • #5600
Issued: 1996 • Retired: 1999
Market Value: $37

Bears

	Date Purchased	Price Paid	Value
44.			
45.			
46.			
47.			
48.			
49.			
50.			
Totals			

51

Forest™
12" • Bear • #5114
Issued: 1998 • Retired: 1998
Market Value: $15

52

Fuzzy™
13" • Bear • #5204
Issued: 1996 • Retired: 1997
Market Value: $70

53

Ginger™
18" • Bear • #5306
Issued: 1997 • Retired: 1997
Market Value: $45

54

Honey™
14" • Bear • #5004
Issued: 1991 • Retired: 1994
A. Blue Ribbon (1992-94)
B. Red Ribbon (1991)
Market Value: A/B–$235

55

Hope™
10" • Bear • #5601
Issued: 1996 • Retired: 1998
Market Value: $23

56

Jumbo PJ™
40" • Bear • #9016
Issued: 1994 • Retired: 1994
Market Value: $475

57

Jumbo PJ™
40" • Bear • #9020
Issued: 1992 • Retired: 1998
Market Value: $200

Bears

	Date Purchased	Price Paid	Value
51.			
52.			
53.			
54.			
55.			
56.			
57.			
Totals			

58

Jumbo Pumpkin™
40" • Bear • #9017
Issued: 1995 • Retired: 1996
Market Value: $525

59

Jumbo Rumples™
40" • Bear • #9016
Issued: 1995 • Retired: 1996
Market Value: $180

60

Jumbo Shaggy™
40" • Bear • #9016
Issued: 1992 • Retired: 1993
Market Value: $600

61

Jumbo Shaggy™
40" • Bear • #9017
Issued: 1992 • Retired: 1994
Market Value: $600

62

Jumbo Shaggy™
40" • Bear • #9026
Issued: 1993 • Retired: 1996
Market Value: $425

63

Kasey™
20" • Koala • #5006
Issued: 1989 • Retired: 1991
A. 20"/Gray (1990-91)
B. 13"/Brown (1989)
Market Value: A–$625 B–$950

Bears

	Date Purchased	Price Paid	Value
58.			
59.			
60.			
61.			
62.			
63.			
Totals			

64

Large Curly™
26" • Bear • #9018
Issued: 1992 • Retired: 1997
Market Value: $85

65

Large Curly™
(moved from Attic Treasures™ in 2000)
26" • Bear • #9019 • Issued: 1992 • Current
A. Flower Sweater, Ty Classic Swing Tag (2000-Current)
B. Flag Sweater, Attic Treasures Swing Tag (1999-2000)
C. Flag Sweater, Ty Plush Swing Tag (1998-99)
D. Ribbon, Ty Plush Swing Tag (1992-98)
Market Value: A–$_____ B–$55 C–$40 D–$30

66

Large Ginger™
22" • Bear • #9027
Issued: 1997 • Retired: 1997
Market Value: $65

67

Large Honey™
26" • Bear • #9021
Issued: 1992 • Retired: 1994
Market Value: $260

68

Large McGee™
26" • Bear • #9005
Issued: 1992 • Retired: 1997
Market Value: $150

69

Large Moonbeam™
20" • Bear • #9009
Issued: 1995 • Retired: 1995
Market Value: $235

70

Large Paws™
28" • Bear • #9029
Issued: 1997 • Current
Market Value: $_____

Bears

	Date Purchased	Price Paid	Value
64.			
65.			
66.			
67.			
68.			
69.			
70.			
Totals			

71

Large Paws™
28" • Bear • #9030
Issued: 1997 • Current
Market Value: $_____

72

Large Paws™
28" • Bear • #9031
Issued: 1998 • Current
Market Value: $_____

73

Large Ping Pong™
26" • Panda • #9010
Issued: 1992 • Retired: 1993
Market Value: $800

74

Large PJ™
26" • Bear • #9012
Issued: 1992 • Retired: 1998
A. 26" (1993-98)
B. 24" (1992)
Market Value: A–$52 B–N/E

75

Large PJ™
26" • Bear • #9014
Issued: 1994 • Retired: 1994
Market Value: $280

76

Large Powder™
22" • Bear • #9028
Issued: 1997 • Retired: 1997
Market Value: $75

77

Large Pumpkin™
26" • Bear • #9015
Issued: 1995 • Retired: 1996
Market Value: $260

Bears

	Date Purchased	Price Paid	Value
71.			
72.			
73.			
74.			
75.			
76.			
77.			
Totals			

78

Large Rumples™
26" • Bear • #9000
Issued: 1995 • Retired: 1995
Market Value: $154

79

Large Rumples™
26" • Bear • #9002
Issued: 1995 • Retired: 1996
Market Value: $110

80

Large Scruffy™
28" • Bear • #9000
Issued: 1992 • Retired: 1993
Market Value: $225

81

Large Scruffy™
28" • Bear • #9013
Issued: 1992 • Retired: 1992
Market Value: $300

82

Large Shaggy™
26" • Bear • #9014
Issued: 1992 • Retired: 1993
Market Value: $350

83

Large Shaggy™
26" • Bear • #9015
Issued: 1993 • Retired: 1994
Market Value: $340

84

Large Shaggy™
26" • Bear • #9025
Issued: 1993 • Retired: 1996
Market Value: $200

Bears

	Date Purchased	Price Paid	Value
78.			
79.			
80.			
81.			
82.			
83.			
84.			
Totals			

85

Large Snowball™
26" • Bear • #9009
Issued: 1992 • Retired: 1993
Market Value: $260

86

Lazy™
20" • Bear • #5008
Issued: 1995 • Retired: 1996
Market Value: $75

87

New!

Lilacbeary™
15" • Bear • #5314
Issued: 2000 • Current
Market Value: $_____

88

Magee™
10" • Bear • #5027
Issued: 1998 • Current
Market Value: $_____

89

Mandarin™
13" • Panda • #5201
Issued: 1996 • Retired: 1997
Market Value: $93

90

McGee™
14" • Bear • #5001
Issued: 1988 • Retired: 1997
A. 14" (1991-97)
B. 13" (1988-90)
Market Value: A–$72 B–$1,000

	Date Purchased	Price Paid	Value
Bears			
85.			
86.			
87.			
88.			
89.			
90.			
Totals			

Ty Classic™

91

Midnight™
20" • Bear • #5009
Issued: 1990 • Retired: 1993
A. Black & Brown (1991, 1993)
B. All Black (1990)
Market Value: A/B–$500

92

Midnight™
13" • Bear • #5101
Issued: 1996 • Retired: 1996
Market Value: $65

93

Moonbeam™
14" • Bear • #5009
Issued: 1995 • Retired: 1995
Market Value: $160

94

Nutmeg™
18" • Bear • #5013
Issued: 1996 • Retired: 1997
Market Value: $55

95

Oreo™
20" • Panda • #5005
Issued: 1994 • Retired: 1996
Market Value: $100

96

Oreo™
20" • Panda • #5010
Issued: 1990 • Retired: 1991
Market Value: $450

97

Papa PJ™
50" • Bear • #9021
Issued: 1997 • Retired: 1998
Market Value: $225

Bears

	Date Purchased	Price Paid	Value
91.			
92.			
93.			
94.			
95.			
96.			
97.			
Totals			

Papa Pumpkin™
50" • Bear • #9023
Issued: 1995 • Retired: 1996
Market Value: $1,200

Papa Rumples™
50" • Bear • #9022
Issued: 1995 • Retired: 1996
Market Value: $800

Papa Shaggy™
50" • Bear • #9024
Issued: 1994 • Retired: 1996
Market Value: $1,200

Paws™
18" • Bear • #5024
Issued: 1997 • Current
Market Value: $_____

Paws™
18" • Bear • #5025
Issued: 1997 • Current
Market Value: $_____

Paws™
18" • Bear • #5026
Issued: 1998 • Current
Market Value: $_____

Ping Pong™
14" • Panda • #5005
Issued: 1989 • Retired: 1993
A. 14" (1991-93)
B. 13" (1989-90)
Market Value: A–$300 B–$860

Bears

	Date Purchased	Price Paid	Value
98.			
99.			
100.			
101.			
102.			
103.			
104.			
Totals			

105

Ping Pong™
N/A • Panda • #5007
Issued: 1989 • Retired: 1989
Market Value: N/E

106

PJ™
18" • Bear • #5200
Issued: 1994 • Retired: 1994
Market Value: $135

107

PJ™
18" • Bear • #5400
Issued: 1991 • Retired: 1998
A. 18" (1993-98)
B. 22" (1991-92)
Market Value: A–$30 B–N/E

108

Powder™
18" • Bear • #5307
Issued: 1997 • Retired: 1997
Market Value: $55

109

Prayer Bear™
14" • Bear • #5600
Issued: 1992 • Retired: 1994
Market Value: $190

110

Prayer Bear™
14" • Bear • #5601
Issued: 1992 • Retired: 1993
Market Value: $230

111

Pudgy™
14" • Bear • #5006
Issued: 1994 • Retired: 1996
Market Value: $175

Bears

	Date Purchased	Price Paid	Value
105.			
106.			
107.			
108.			
109.			
110.			
111.			
Totals			

112

Pumpkin™
18" • Bear • #5304
Issued: 1995 • Retired: 1996
Market Value: $155

113

Purplebeary™
14" • Bear • #5313
Issued: 1999 • Current
Market Value: $_____

114

Rags™
12" • Bear • #5102
Issued: 1992 • Retired: 1996
Market Value: $75

115

Romeo™
14" • Bear • #5310
Issued: 1998 • Current
A. Gold Ribbon/I Love You (1998-Current)
B. Purple Ribbon/Mother's Day (1998)
C. Red Ribbon (1998)
Market Value: A–$_____ B–$22 C–N/E

116

Ruffles™
12" • Bear • #5014
Issued: 1995 • Retired: 1995
Market Value: $120

117

Rufus™
18" • Bear • #5015
Issued: 1993 • Retired: 1997
Market Value: $94

Bears

	Date Purchased	Price Paid	Value
112.			
113.			
114.			
115.			
116.			
117.			
Totals			

Ty Classic™

118

Rumples™
18" • Bear • #5002
Issued: 1995 • Retired: 1996
Market Value: $65

119

Rumples™
18" • Bear • #5003
Issued: 1995 • Retired: 1995
A. Brown Nose/Green Ribbon (1995)
B. Pink Nose/Pink Ribbon (1995)
Market Value: A/B–$120

120

Sam™
18" • Bear • #5010
Issued: 1995 • Retired: 1996
Market Value: $170

121

Scruffy™
18" • Bear • #5012
Issued: 1991 • Retired: 1994
Market Value: $125

122

Scruffy™
18" • Bear • #5013
Issued: 1992 • Retired: 1995
A. Gold (1995)
B. Cream (1992)
Market Value: A–$120 B–$200

123

Shadow™
20" • Bear • #5011
Issued: 1994 • Retired: 1996
Market Value: $118

124

Shaggy™
18" • Bear • #5303
Issued: 1992 • Retired: 1993
A. 18" (1993)
B. 24" (1992)
Market Value: A/B–$216

Bears

	Date Purchased	Price Paid	Value
118.			
119.			
120.			
121.			
122.			
123.			
124.			
Totals			

125

Shaggy™
18" • Bear • #5304
Issued: 1992 • Retired: 1994
Market Value: $220

126

Shaggy™
18" • Bear • #5305
Issued: 1993 • Retired: 1996
Market Value: $105

127

Snowball™
14" • Bear • #5002
Issued: 1988 • Retired: 1993
A. 14"/Red Ribbon (1991-93)
B. 13"/Red Ribbon (1990)
C. 13"/Blue Ribbon (1989)
D. 13"/No Ribbon (1988)
**Market Value: A–$185 B–N/E
C–$775 D–N/E**

128

Spice™
18" • Bear • #5020
Issued: 1996 • Retired: 1997
Market Value: $40

129

Sugar™
14" • Bear • #5007
Issued: 1995 • Retired: 1995
Market Value: $80

130

Sugar™
14" • Polar Bear • #5008
Issued: 1990 • Retired: 1991
A. 14" (1991)
B. 20" (1990)
Market Value: A/B–$320

131

Super Buddy™
32" • Bear • #9006
Issued: 1990 • Retired: 1991
Market Value: $990

Bears

	Date Purchased	Price Paid	Value
125.			
126.			
127.			
128.			
129.			
130.			
131.			
Totals			

171

Ty Classic™

132

Super McGee™
26" • Bear • #9005
Issued: 1991 • Retired: 1991
Market Value: N/E

133

Super Ping Pong™
26" • Panda • #9010
Issued: 1991 • Retired: 1991
Market Value: N/E

134

Super PJ™
24" • Bear • #9012
Issued: 1991 • Retired: 1991
Market Value: N/E

135

Super Scruffy™
28" • Bear • #9000
Issued: 1991 • Retired: 1991
Market Value: $370

136

Super Snowball™
26" • Bear • #9009
Issued: 1991 • Retired: 1991
Market Value: N/E

137

New!

Taffybeary™
15" • Bear • #5315
Issued: 2000 • Current
Market Value: $____

Bears

	Date Purchased	Price Paid	Value
132.			
133.			
134.			
135.			
136.			
137.			
138.			
Totals			

138

Theodore™
19" • Bear • #5501
Issued: 1996 • Retired: 1997
Market Value: $93

139

Vanilla™
18" • Bear • #5012
Issued: 1996 • Retired: 1997
Market Value: $65

140

Wuzzy™
13" • Bear • #5202
Issued: 1996 • Retired: 1997
Market Value: $80

141

New!

Yesterbear™
18" • Bear • #5028
Issued: 2000 • Current
Market Value: $_____

142

New!

Yesterbear™
18" • Bear • #5029
Issued: 2000 • Current
Market Value: $_____

143

New!

Yesterbear™
18" • Bear • #5030
Issued: 2000 • Current
Market Value: $_____

144

PHOTO UNAVAILABLE

Yukon™
N/A • Bear • #7424
Issued: 1996 • Retired: 1996
Market Value: $125

Bears

	Date Purchased	Price Paid	Value
139.			
140.			
141.			
142.			
143.			
144.			
Totals			

Ty Classic™

Cats

In 1986, Ty Warner began selling a line of stuffed Himalayan cats and has watched the family grow to 52 kitties. Take note – most of the cats are retired, so be sure to add the new ones to your collection before they're gone!

145

Al E. Kat™
22" • Cat • #1111
Issued: 1988 • Current
A. 22"/Curled (1996-Current)
B. 20"/Curled (1992-95)
C. 20"/Flat (1989-91)
D. 23"/Flat (1988)
Market Value: A– $_____ B– N/E C– $150 D– $800

146

Al E. Kat™
22" • Cat • #1112
Issued: 1989 • Retired: 1998
A. 22"/Curled (1996-98)
B. 20"/Curled (1992-95)
C. 20"/Flat (1989-91)
Market Value: A– $26 B– $300 C– $150

147

Angel™
20" • Persian • #1001
Issued: 1988 • Retired: 1995
Market Value: $70

148

Angel™
20" • Himalayan • #1001H
Issued: 1988 • Retired: 1990
Market Value: $1,000

149

Angel™
17" • Persian • #1122
Issued: 1998 • Retired: 1998
Market Value: $24

150

Angora™
N/A • Cat • #1001
Issued: 1986 • Retired: 1986
Market Value: N/E

Cats

	Date Purchased	Price Paid	Value
145.			
146.			
147.			
148.			
149.			
150.			
Totals			

151

Baby Angora™
N/A • Cat • #1002
Issued: 1986 • Retired: 1986
Market Value: N/E

152

Baby Bijan™
N/A • Cat • #1006
Issued: 1986 • Retired: 1986
Market Value: $1,000

153

Baby Butterball™
N/A • Cat • #2006
Issued: 1986 • Retired: 1986
Market Value: $1,300

154

Baby Jasmine™
N/A • Cat • #1004
Issued: 1986 • Retired: 1986
Market Value: $1,200

155

Baby Kasha™
N/A • Cat • #1008
Issued: 1986 • Retired: 1986
Market Value: $1,200

156

PHOTO UNAVAILABLE

Baby Kimchi™
N/A • Cat • #2004
Issued: 1986 • Retired: 1986
Market Value: $1,350

157

Baby Oscar™
N/A • Cat • #2008
Issued: 1986 • Retired: 1986
Market Value: $1,275

Cats

	Date Purchased	Price Paid	Value
151.			
152.			
153.			
154.			
155.			
156.			
157.			
Totals			

158

Baby Snowball™
N/A • Cat • #2002
Issued: 1986 • Retired: 1986
Market Value: $1,200

159

Bijan™
N/A • Cat • #1005
Issued: 1986 • Retired: 1986
Market Value: $1,200

160

Boots™
16" • Cat • #1123
Issued: 1998 • Current
Market Value: $_____

161

Butterball™
N/A • Cat • #2005
Issued: 1986 • Retired: 1986
Market Value: $1,200

162

Coal™
16" • Cat • #1119
Issued: 1997 • Retired: 1997
Market Value: $65

163

Crystal™
16" • Cat • #1120
Issued: 1997 • Retired: 1999
Market Value: $15

164

Fluffy™
15" • Persian • #1002
Issued: 1996 • Retired: 1997
Market Value: $38

Cats

	Date Purchased	Price Paid	Value
158.			
159.			
160.			
161.			
162.			
163.			
164.			
Totals			

165

Frisky™
17" • Cat • #1007
Issued: 1996 • Retired: 1997
Market Value: $70

166

Ginger™
20" • Cat • #1007
Issued: 1988 • Retired: 1990
Market Value: $475

167

Ginger™
20" • Himalayan • #1007H
Issued: 1988 • Retired: 1990
Market Value: $1,150

168

Jasmine™
N/A • Cat • #1003
Issued: 1986 • Retired: 1986
Market Value: $1,000

169

Kasha™
N/A • Cat • #1007
Issued: 1986 • Retired: 1986
Market Value: $1,000

170

Kimchi™
N/A • Cat • #2003
Issued: 1986 • Retired: 1986
Market Value: $1,000

Cats

	Date Purchased	Price Paid	Value
165.			
166.			
167.			
168.			
169.			
170.			
Totals			

Ty Classic™

171

Licorice™
20" • Persian • #1009
Issued: 1988 • Retired: 1995
Market Value: $170

172

Licorice™
17" • Persian • #1125
Issued: 1998 • Retired: 1998
Market Value: $17

173

Maggie™
22" • Cat • #1115
Issued: 1992 • Retired: 1998
A. 22"/Curled (1996-98)
B. 20"/Flat (1992-95)
Market Value: A–$42 B–$130

174

Mittens™
12" • Cat • #1117
Issued: 1993 • Retired: 1994
Market Value: $190

175

Mittens™
12" • Cat • #1118
Issued: 1993 • Retired: 1994
Market Value: $190

176

New!

Mystery™
13" • Cat • #1127
Issued: 2000 • Current
Market Value: $_____

Cats

	Date Purchased	Price Paid	Value
171.			
172.			
173.			
174.			
175.			
176.			
177.			
Totals			

177

Oscar™
N/A • Cat • #2007
Issued: 1986 • Retired: 1986
Market Value: $1,200

Value Guide — Ty® Plush Animals

Patches™
20" • Cat • #1114
Issued: 1991 • Retired: 1995
Market Value: $135

Peaches™
20" • Cat • #1003
Issued: 1988 • Retired: 1993
Market Value: $400

Peaches™
20" • Himalayan • #1003H
Issued: 1988 • Retired: 1990
Market Value: $1,200

New!

Prissy™
13" • Cat • #1128
Issued: 2000 • Current
Market Value: $_____

Puffy™
15" • Persian • #1003
Issued: 1996 • Retired: 1997
Market Value: $42

Scratch™
15" • Cat • #1117
Issued: 1996 • Retired: 1997
Market Value: $85

Screech™
15" • Cat • #1116
Issued: 1995 • Retired: 1996
A. Collar (1996)
B. No Collar (1995)
Market Value: A/B–$94

Cats

	Date Purchased	Price Paid	Value
178.			
179.			
180.			
181.			
182.			
183.			
184.			
Totals			

Ty Classic™

185

Shadow™
20" • Cat • #1112
Issued: 1988 • Retired: 1988
Market Value: $1,000

186

New!

Shadow™
13" • Cat • #1129
Issued: 2000 • Current
Market Value: $_____

187

Sherlock™
20" • Cat • #1110
Issued: 1990 • Retired: 1992
Market Value: $450

188

Silky™
15" • Persian • #1004
Issued: 1996 • Retired: 1997
Market Value: $45

189

Smokey™
20" • Cat • #1005
Issued: 1988 • Retired: 1993
Market Value: $345

190

Smokey™
20" • Himalayan • #1005H
Issued: 1988 • Retired: 1990
Market Value: $1,150

191

New!

Smokey™
16" • Cat • #1130
Issued: 2000 • Current
Market Value: $_____

Cats

	Date Purchased	Price Paid	Value
185.			
186.			
187.			
188.			
189.			
190.			
191.			
Totals			

192

Snowball™
N/A • Cat • #2001
Issued: 1986 • Retired: 1986
Market Value: $1,200

193

Socks™
12" • Cat • #1116
Issued: 1993 • Retired: 1994
Market Value: $185

194

Spice™
17" • Cat • #1121
Issued: 1998 • Current
Market Value: $_____

195

New!

Stretch™
14" • Cat • #1131
Issued: 2000 • Current
Market Value: $_____

196

Tumbles™
17" • Cat • #1008
Issued: 1996 • Retired: 1997
Market Value: $80

Cats

	Date Purchased	Price Paid	Value
192.			
193.			
194.			
195.			
196.			
Totals			

Ty Classic™

Dogs

Three new dogs joined the litter in 2000, bringing the Ty pooch total to 60. There's something for everyone in this collection, so if you'd like to romp with a retriever or prance with a poodle, you're sure to find a new best friend here.

197

Ace™
12" • Dalmatian • #2027
Issued: 1998 • Retired: 1998
Market Value: $15

198

Ashes™
8" • Labrador Retriever • #2018
Issued: 1996 • Retired: 1996
Market Value: $45

199

Baby Patches™
12" • Dog • #2030
Issued: 1999 • Current
Market Value: $_____

200

Baby Schnapps™
N/A • Dog • #3001
Issued: 1986 • Retired: 1986
Market Value: N/E

201

Baby Sparky™
20" • Dalmatian • #2012
Issued: 1992 • Retired: 1994
A. Tongue (1994)
B. No Tongue (1992-93)
Market Value: A/B–$135

202

Barney™
20" • Labrador Retriever • #2003
Issued: 1990 • Retired: 1992
Market Value: $800

Dogs

	Date Purchased	Price Paid	Value
197.			
198.			
199.			
200.			
201.			
202.			
Totals			

203

Biscuit™
17" • Dog • #2026
Issued: 1997 • Retired: 1997
Market Value: $45

204

Bo™
20" • Basset Hound • #2009
Issued: 1994 • Retired: 1995
Market Value: $250

205

Buckshot™
20" • Basset Hound • #2009
Issued: 1992 • Retired: 1993
Market Value: $540

206

Buster™
20" • Cocker Spaniel • #2005
Issued: 1990 • Retired: 1991
Market Value: $635

207

Charlie™
20" • Cocker Spaniel • #2001
Issued: 1988 • Retired: 1990
A. Tongue (1990)
B. No Tongue (1988-89)
Market Value: A/B–$900

208

Charlie™
20" • Cocker Spaniel • #2005
Issued: 1994 • Retired: 1997
A. Floppy (1996-97)
B. Sitting (1994-95)
Market Value: A–$45 B–$90

209

Chips™
12" • Dog • #2025
Issued: 1997 • Retired: 1999
Market Value: $16

Dogs

	Date Purchased	Price Paid	Value
203.			
204.			
205.			
206.			
207.			
208.			
209.			
Totals			

Ty Classic™

210

Churchill™
12" • Bulldog • #2017
Issued: 1996 • Retired: 1999
Market Value: $16

211

Cinders™
20" • Labrador Retriever • #2008
Issued: 1994 • Retired: 1997
A. Sitting/Black & Brown (1995-97)
B. Floppy/All Black (1994)
Market Value: A/B–$65

212

Corky™
12" • Cocker Spaniel • #2023
Issued: 1996 • Current
Market Value: $_____

213

Dakota™
12" • Husky • #7418
Issued: 1995 • Current
A. 12"/Floppy (1998-Current)
B. 8"/Sitting (1997)
C. 12"/Sitting (1995-97)
Market Value: A–$_____ B–N/E C–$40

214

Dopey™
17" • Dog • #2022
Issued: 1996 • Retired: 1997
Market Value: $75

215

Droopy™
15" • Hound • #2009
Issued: 1996 • Retired: 1997
Market Value: $50

216

New!

Duster™
17" • Dog • #2031
Issued: 2000 • Current
Market Value: $_____

Dogs

	Date Purchased	Price Paid	Value
210.			
211.			
212.			
213.			
214.			
215.			
216.			
Totals			

217

Elvis™
20" • Hound • #2010
Issued: 1995 • Retired: 1998
Market Value: $43

218

Fido™
8" • Dog • #2019
Issued: 1996 • Retired: 1996
Market Value: $55

219

Fritz™
20" • Dalmatian • #2002
Issued: 1988 • Retired: 1990
A. Tongue (1990)
B. No Tongue (1988-89)
Market Value: A/B–$1,000

220

Honey™
20" • Dog • #2001
Issued: 1995 • Retired: 1998
Market Value: $32

221

PHOTO UNAVAILABLE

Large Max™
N/A • Dog • #9001
Issued: 1992 • Retired: 1992
Market Value: $800

222

Large Rusty™
26" • Mutt • #9011
Issued: 1994 • Retired: 1995
Market Value: $160

223

Large Scruffy™
26" • Dog • #9011
Issued: 1992 • Retired: 1993
Market Value: $230

Dogs

	Date Purchased	Price Paid	Value
217.			
218.			
219.			
220.			
221.			
222.			
223.			
Totals			

Ty Classic™

224

Large Sparky™
26" • Dalmatian • #9002
Issued: 1992 • Retired: 1993
Market Value: $265

225

Max™
20" • Dog • #2008
Issued: 1991 • Retired: 1992
Market Value: $315

226

Max™
20" • Dog • #3001
Issued: 1988 • Retired: 1990
A. Tongue (1990)
B. No Tongue (1988-89)
Market Value: A/B–$850

227

Muffin™
13" • Dog • #2020
Issued: 1996 • Retired: 1998
Market Value: $20

228

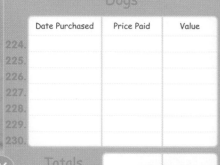

Patches™
18" • Dog • #2003
Issued: 1996 • Current
Market Value: $_____

229

Pepper™
12" • Labrador Retriever • #2024
Issued: 1997 • Retired: 1999
Market Value: $16

230

Pierre™
10" • Poodle • #2004
Issued: 1995 • Retired: 1996
Market Value: $90

Dogs

	Date Purchased	Price Paid	Value
224.			
225.			
226.			
227.			
228.			
229.			
230.			

Totals

231

Rusty™
20" • Mutt • #2011
Issued: 1992 • Retired: 1996
Market Value: $62

232

Sarge™
20" • German Shepherd • #2003
Issued: 1994 • Retired: 1995
Market Value: $335

233

Schnapps™
N/A • Dog • #3000
Issued: 1986 • Retired: 1986
Market Value: $875

234

New!

Scooter™
16" • Dog • #2033
Issued: 2000 • Current
Market Value: $____

235

Scruffy™
20" • Dog • #2000
Issued: 1992 • Retired: 1996
A. Red Ribbon/White (1993-96)
B. Blue Ribbon/Cream (1992)
Market Value: A–$92 B–$180

236

Scruffy™
20" • Dog • #2001
Issued: 1991 • Retired: 1994
A. Ribbon (1992-94)
B. No Ribbon (1991)
Market Value: A/B–$133

237

Sherlock™
12" • Basset Hound • #2029
Issued: 1998 • Retired: 1998
Market Value: $17

Dogs

	Date Purchased	Price Paid	Value
231.			
232.			
233.			
234.			
235.			
236.			
237.			
Totals			

Ty Classic™

238

Sniffles™
18" • Dog • #2021
Issued: 1996 • Retired: 1996
Market Value: $173

239

Spanky™
20" • St. Bernard • #2010
Issued: 1992 • Retired: 1993
Market Value: $300

240

Spanky™
8" • Cocker Spaniel • #2015
Issued: 1996 • Retired: 1996
Market Value: $43

241

Sparky™
20" • Dalmatian • #2004
Issued: 1990 • Retired: 1993
Market Value: $350

242

Sparky™
20" • Dalmatian • #2012
Issued: 1995 • Retired: 1995
Market Value: $150

243

Sunny™
14" • Dog • #2028
Issued: 1998 • Retired: 1998
Market Value: $15

244

Super Fritz™
36" • Dalmatian • #9002
Issued: 1989 • Retired: 1989
Market Value: $1,100

Dogs

	Date Purchased	Price Paid	Value
238.			
239.			
240.			
241.			
242.			
243.			
244.			
Totals			

245

Super Max™
32" • Dog • #3002
Issued: 1988 • Retired: 1990
A. Tongue (1990)
B. No Tongue (1988-89)
Market Value: A/B–$910

246

Super Max™
26" • Dog • #9001
Issued: 1991 • Retired: 1992
A. 26" (1992)
B. 32" (1991)
Market Value: A/B–$600

247

Super Schnapps™
N/A • Dog • #3002
Issued: 1986 • Retired: 1986
Market Value: $1,400

248

Super Scruffy™
32" • Dog • #9011
Issued: 1991 • Retired: 1991
Market Value: $375

249

Super Sparky™
32" • Dalmatian • #9002
Issued: 1990 • Retired: 1991
Market Value: $800

250

Taffy™
12" • Terrier • #2014
Issued: 1996 • Current
A. 12" (1998-Current)
B. 8" (1996-97)
Market Value: A–$_____ B–$35

251

Timber™
20" • Husky • #2002
Issued: 1994 • Retired: 1998
Market Value: $60

Dogs

	Date Purchased	Price Paid	Value
245.			
246.			
247.			
248.			
249.			
250.			
251.			
Totals			

252

Toffee™
20" • Terrier • #2013
Issued: 1993 • Retired: 1999
Market Value: $50

253

New!

Toffee™
20" • Dog • #2032
Issued: 2000 • Current
Market Value: $_____

254

Winston™
20" • Bulldog • #2007
Issued: 1991 • Retired: 1999
Market Value: $35

255

Yappy™
12" • Yorkshire Terrier • #2016
Issued: 1996 • Current
A. 12" (1998-Current)
B. 8" (1996-97)
Market Value: A–$_____ B–$40

256

Yorkie™
20" • Yorkshire Terrier • #2006
Issued: 1991 • Retired: 1996
Market Value: $94

Dogs

	Date Purchased	Price Paid	Value
252.			
253.			
254.			
255.			
256.			
Totals			

190

Country

A bunny named "Peter" was the only animal to join the country critters in January 2000. With the addition of "Peter," there are currently 56 country dwellers of all kinds, including cows, pigs and sheep, among others.

257

Angora™
14" • Rabbit • #8004
Issued: 1995 • Retired: 1995
Market Value: $150

258

Angora™
20" • Rabbit • #8005
Issued: 1991 • Retired: 1992
Market Value: $400

259

Arnold™
20" • Pig • #6001
Issued: 1988 • Retired: 1989
Market Value: $1,000

260

Arnold™
20" • Pig • #6002
Issued: 1990 • Retired: 1990
Market Value: $410

261

Baby Clover™
12" • Cow • #8023
Issued: 1993 • Retired: 1994
Market Value: $100

Country

	Date Purchased	Price Paid	Value
257.			
258.			
259.			
260.			
261.			
Totals			

262

Baby Curly Bunny™
12" • Bunny • #8024
Issued: 1993 • Retired: 1997
Market Value: $42

263

Baby Curly Bunny™
12" • Bunny • #8025
Issued: 1993 • Retired: 1997
Market Value: $36

264

Baby Lovie™
20" • Lamb • #8019
Issued: 1992 • Retired: 1992
Market Value: $200

265

Baby Lovie™
12" • Lamb • #8020
Issued: 1993 • Retired: 1994
Market Value: $115

266

Baby Petunia™
12" • Pig • #8021
Issued: 1993 • Retired: 1994
A. Red Ribbon (1994)
B. Blue Ribbon (1993)
Market Value: A/B–$125

267

Baby Pokey™
13" • Rabbit • #8022
Issued: 1996 • Retired: 1997
Market Value: $35

268

Baby Smokey™
13" • Rabbit • #8023
Issued: 1996 • Retired: 1997
Market Value: $35

Country

	Date Purchased	Price Paid	Value
262.			
263.			
264.			
265.			
266.			
267.			
268.			
Totals			

Ty Classic™

269

Bandit™
20" • Raccoon • #1119
Issued: 1990 • Retired: 1990
Market Value: $525

270

Beanie Bunny™
12" • Bunny • #8000
Issued: 1989 • Retired: 1992
Market Value: $725

271

Beanie Bunny™
12" • Bunny • #8001
Issued: 1991 • Retired: 1992
Market Value: $725

272

Big Beanie Bunny™
15" • Bunny • #8011
Issued: 1990 • Retired: 1992
A. Gold Ribbon (1991-92)
B. Pink Ribbon (1990)
Market Value: A/B–N/E

273

Big Beanie Bunny™
15" • Bunny • #8012
Issued: 1991 • Retired: 1992
Market Value: $600

274

Blossom™
18" • Rabbit • #8013
Issued: 1996 • Retired: 1997
Market Value: $80

275

Bows™
11" • Bunny • #8030
Issued: 1998 • Retired: 1999
Market Value: $16

Country

	Date Purchased	Price Paid	Value
269.			
270.			
271.			
272.			
273.			
274.			
275.			
Totals			

276

Buttercup™
18" • Rabbit • #8012
Issued: 1996 • Retired: 1997
Market Value: $95

277

Buttons™
11" • Bunny • #8031
Issued: 1998 • Retired: 1999
Market Value: $15

278

Candy™
N/A • Rabbit • #8011
Issued: 1996 • Retired: 1996
Market Value: $80

279

Chestnut™
12" • Squirrel • #8022
Issued: 1993 • Retired: 1993
Market Value: $170

280

Clover™
20" • Cow • #8007
Issued: 1991 • Retired: 1996
A. Ribbon (1996) B. No Ribbon (1994-95)
C. Ribbon (1991-93)
Market Value: A/B/C–$127

281

Cotton™
14" • Rabbit • #8003
Issued: 1996 • Retired: 1997
Market Value: $43

Country		
Date Purchased	Price Paid	Value
276.		
277.		
278.		
279.		
280.		
281.		
Totals		

282

Curly Bunny™
(moved from Attic Treasures™ in 2000)
22" • Bunny • #8017 • Issued: 1992 • Current
A. Sweater, Ty Classic Swing Tag (2000-Current)
B. Sweater, Attic Treasures Swing Tag (1999-2000)
C. Sweater, Ty Plush Swing Tag (1998-99)
D. No Clothes, Ty Plush Swing Tag (1992-98)
Market Value: A– $_____ B– $45 C– $25 D– $20

283

Curly Bunny™
(moved from Attic Treasures™ in 2000)
22" • Bunny • #8018 • Issued: 1992 • Current
A. Sweater, Ty Classic Swing Tag (2000-Current)
B. Sweater, Attic Treasures Swing Tag (1999-2000)
C. Sweater, Ty Plush Swing Tag (1998-99)
D. No Clothes, Ty Plush Swing Tag (1992-98)
Market Value: A– $_____ B– $45 C– $25 D– $20

284

Domino™
20" • Rabbit • #8006
Issued: 1991 • Retired: 1992
Market Value: $420

285

Freddie™
12" • Frog • #1117
Issued: 1989 • Retired: 1990
A. 12" (1990) B. 10" (1989)
Market Value: A– N/E B– $1,100

286

Freddie™
N/A • Frog • #8002
Issued: 1989 • Retired: 1989
Market Value: N/E

287

Hooters™
9" • Owl • #8016
Issued: 1992 • Retired: 1994
Market Value: $350

288

Jersey™
20" • Cow • #8026
Issued: 1997 • Retired: 1998
A. Black & White (1997-98)
B. Brown & White (1997)
Market Value: A– $24 B– $45

Country

	Date Purchased	Price Paid	Value
282.			
283.			
284.			
285.			
286.			
287.			
288.			
Totals			

Ty Classic™

289

Large Curly Bunny™
24" • Bunny • #9003
Issued: 1994 • Retired: 1997
Market Value: $80

290

Large Curly Bunny™
24" • Bunny • #9007
Issued: 1996 • Retired: 1997
Market Value: $70

291

Large Petunia™
26" • Pig • #9003
Issued: 1992 • Retired: 1992
Market Value: $500

292

Lillie™
20" • Lamb • #8004
Issued: 1990 • Retired: 1990
Market Value: $510

293
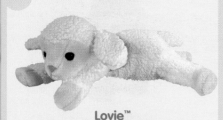

Lovie™
18" • Lamb • #8001
Issued: 1988 • Retired: 1990
Market Value: $625

294

Lovie™
20" • Lamb • #8004
Issued: 1991 • Retired: 1993
Market Value: $430

295

Lovie™
20" • Lamb • #8019
Issued: 1993 • Retired: 1996
Market Value: $125

Country

	Date Purchased	Price Paid	Value
289.			
290.			
291.			
292.			
293.			
294.			
295.			
Totals			

296

Lovie™
10" • Lamb • #8027
Issued: 1998 • Retired: 1999
Market Value: $28

297

Nibbles™
9" • Bunny • #8000
Issued: 1994 • Retired: 1999
Market Value: $12

298

Nibbles™
9" • Bunny • #8001
Issued: 1995 • Retired: 1999
Market Value: $12

299

Peepers™
9" • Chick • #8015
Issued: 1991 • Retired: 1994
A. Feet (1992-94) B. No Feet (1991)
Market Value: A/B–$180

300

Peter™
14" • Rabbit • #8002
Issued: 1989 • Retired: 1997
A. 14"/Jointed (1996-97)
B. 20"/Not Jointed (1989-94)
Market Value: A–$60 B–$400

301

New!

Peter™
15" • Bunny • #8020
Issued: 2000 • Current
Market Value: $_____

Country

	Date Purchased	Price Paid	Value
296.			
297.			
298.			
299.			
300.			
301.			
Totals			

Ty Classic™

Petunia™
20" • Pig • #6001
Issued: 1989 • Retired: 1990
Market Value: $520

Petunia™
20" • Pig • #8008
Issued: 1991 • Retired: 1995
A. Red Ribbon (1994-95)
B. Blue Ribbon (1993)
C. Pink Ribbon (1991-92)
Market Value: A–$160 B–$170 C–$175

Pokey™
19" • Rabbit • #8015
Issued: 1996 • Retired: 1997
Market Value: $55

Rosie™
20" • Rabbit • #8003
Issued: 1990 • Retired: 1994
Market Value: $440

Smokey™
19" • Rabbit • #8016
Issued: 1996 • Retired: 1997
Market Value: $50

Sparkles™
20" • Unicorn • #8100
Issued: 1997 • Current
A. Multi-Color Mane & Tail (1999-Current)
B. Pink Mane & Tail (1997-98)
Market Value: A–$_____ B–N/E

Super Arnold™
32" • Pig • #9003
Issued: 1990 • Retired: 1990
Market Value: $980

Country

	Date Purchased	Price Paid	Value
302.			
303.			
304.			
305.			
306.			
307.			
308.			
Totals			

309

Super Petunia™
32" • Pig • #9003
Issued: 1989 • Retired: 1991
A. 32"/Ribbon (1991)
B. 36"/No Ribbon (1989)
Market Value: A/B–N/E

310

Tulip™
18" • Pig • #8008
Issued: 1996 • Retired: 1998
Market Value: $45

311

Whinnie™
20" • Horse • #8006
Issued: 1994 • Retired: 1995
Market Value: $260

312

Woolly™
9" • Lamb • #8005
Issued: 1996 • Retired: 1999
Market Value: $12

Country

	Date Purchased	Price Paid	Value
309.			
310.			
311.			
312.			
Totals			

Wildlife

Explore the wilds of *Ty Classic* with this collection of monkeys, lions, leopards, chimpanzees and much more. Four new wild animals just joined the group, bringing the total number to 70.

313

Arctic™
12" • Polar Bear • #7419
Issued: 1995 • Retired: 1997
Market Value: $58

314

Baby George™
12" • Gorilla • #7300
Issued: 1996 • Retired: 1998
Market Value: $16

315

Bandit™
20" • Raccoon • #8009
Issued: 1991 • Retired: 1996
A. Brown (1992-96)
B. Gray (1991)
Market Value: A–$100 B–$850

316

Bengal™
12" • Tiger • #7423
Issued: 1995 • Current
A. Floppy/Gold Chest (1998-Current)
B. Sitting/White Chest (1995-97)
Market Value: A–$_____ B–$46

317

Big George™
27" • Gorilla • #7302
Issued: 1990 • Current
Market Value: $_____

Wildlife

	Date Purchased	Price Paid	Value
313.			
314.			
315.			
316.			
317.			
Totals			

318

Big Jake™
16" • Monkey • #7002
Issued: 1989 • Retired: 1989
Market Value: $500

319

Big Jake™
16" • Monkey • #7002A
Issued: 1989 • Retired: 1989
Market Value: $510

320

Big Jake™
16" • Monkey • #7002C
Issued: 1989 • Retired: 1989
Market Value: $510

321

Big Jake™
16" • Monkey • #7200
Issued: 1990 • Retired: 1990
Market Value: $500

322

Big Jake™
16" • Monkey • #7201
Issued: 1990 • Retired: 1990
Market Value: $500

323

Big Jake™
16" • Monkey • #7202
Issued: 1990 • Retired: 1990
Market Value: $800

Wildlife

	Date Purchased	Price Paid	Value
318.			
319.			
320.			
321.			
322.			
323.			
Totals			

324

Cha Cha™
12" • Monkey • #7005
Issued: 1998 • Current
Market Value: $_____

325

Chi-Chi™
20" • Cheetah • #1114
Issued: 1989 • Retired: 1990
A. No Ribbon (1990) B. Ribbon (1989)
Market Value: A/B–$950

326

Chi-Chi™
20" • Cheetah • #7414
Issued: 1991 • Retired: 1992
Market Value: $580

327

Chuckles™
15" • Chimp • #7303
Issued: 1997 • Retired: 1997
Market Value: $55

328

New!

Dash™
14" • Tiger • #7432
Issued: 2000 • Current
Market Value: $_____

329

New!

Dot™
14" • Leopard • #7433
Issued: 2000 • Current
Market Value: $_____

Wildlife

	Date Purchased	Price Paid	Value
324.			
325.			
326.			
327.			
328.			
329.			
Totals			

330

Elmer™
20" • Elephant • #1116
Issued: 1989 • Retired: 1990
A. No Ribbon (1990) B. Ribbon (1989)
Market Value: A/B–$770

331

Elmer™
20" • Elephant • #7416
Issued: 1991 • Retired: 1996
A. Gray Ears/Long Trunk (1994-96)
B. White Ears/Short Trunk (1991-93)
Market Value: A–$115   B–$300

332

Freddie™
16" • Frog • #8010
Issued: 1991 • Retired: 1998
A. 16" (1995-98)
B. 12" (1991)
Market Value: A–$40   B–N/E

333

George™
20" • Gorilla • #7301
Issued: 1990 • Retired: 1999
Market Value: N/E

334

Harris™
20" • Lion • #1115
Issued: 1989 • Retired: 1990
A. Gold & Tan Mane (1990)
B. Gold Mane (1989)
Market Value: A/B–$700

335

Harris™
20" • Lion • #7415
Issued: 1991 • Retired: 1996
Market Value: $85

336

Jake™
12" • Monkey • #7001
Issued: 1988 • Retired: 1989
Market Value: $650

Wildlife

	Date Purchased	Price Paid	Value
330.			
331.			
332.			
333.			
334.			
335.			
336.			
Totals			

337

Jake™
12" • Monkey • #7001A
Issued: 1989 • Retired: 1989
Market Value: $650

338

Jake™
N/A • Monkey • #7001B
Issued: 1989 • Retired: 1989
Market Value: $500

339

Jake™
12" • Monkey • #7001C
Issued: 1989 • Retired: 1989
Market Value: $650

340

Jake™
N/A • Monkey • #7001R
Issued: 1989 • Retired: 1989
Market Value: N/E

341

Jake™
24" • Monkey • #7100
Issued: 1990 • Retired: 1994
A. 24" (1992-94) B. 22" (1991) C. 12" (1990)
Market Value: A–$270 B–N/E C–N/E

342

Jake™
24" • Monkey • #7101
Issued: 1990 • Retired: 1993
A. 24" (1992-93) B. 22" (1991) C. 12" (1990)
Market Value: A–$430 B–N/E C–N/E

343

Jake™
12" • Monkey • #7102
Issued: 1990 • Retired: 1990
Market Value: $800

Wildlife

	Date Purchased	Price Paid	Value
337.			
338.			
339.			
340.			
341.			
342.			
343.			
Totals			

344

New!

Jake™
18" • Gorilla • #7434
Issued: 2000 • Current
Market Value: $_____

345

Josh™
24" • Monkey • #7101
Issued: 1994 • Retired: 1996
Market Value: $125

346

Jumbo George™
48" • Gorilla • #9008
Issued: 1991 • Current
Market Value: $_____

347

Leo™
22" • Lion • #7427
Issued: 1997 • Retired: 1998
Market Value: $26

348

Mango™
20" • Monkey • #7100
Issued: 1995 • Retired: 1998
Market Value: $24

349

Mango™
20" • Monkey • #7102
Issued: 1995 • Retired: 1998
Market Value: $24

Wildlife

	Date Purchased	Price Paid	Value
344.			
345.			
346.			
347.			
348.			
349.			
Totals			

350

Mischief™
18" • Monkey • #7000
Issued: 1988 • Retired: 1993
A. White (1991-93) B. Auburn (1990)
C. White (1988-89)
Market Value: A–$360 B–N/E C–$360

351

Mischief™
18" • Monkey • #7000A
Issued: 1989 • Retired: 1989
Market Value: $400

352

Mischief™
N/A • Monkey • #7000B
Issued: 1989 • Retired: 1989
Market Value: $400

353

Mischief™
18" • Monkey • #7000C
Issued: 1989 • Retired: 1989
Market Value: $425

354

Mischief™
N/A • Monkey • #7000R
Issued: 1989 • Retired: 1989
Market Value: N/E

355

Mischief™
18" • Monkey • #7001
Issued: 1990 • Retired: 1993
A. Auburn (1991-93) B. White (1990)
Market Value: A–$320 B–$350

356

Mischief™
18" • Monkey • #7002
Issued: 1990 • Retired: 1991
Market Value: $350

Wildlife

	Date Purchased	Price Paid	Value
350.			
351.			
352.			
353.			
354.			
355.			
356.			
Totals			

357

Mischief™
21" • Monkey • #7414
Issued: 1996 • Retired: 1997
Market Value: $100

358

Misty™
14" • Seal • #7400
Issued: 1991 • Retired: 1994
A. 14"/Ribbon (1993-94)
B. 12"/No Ribbon (1991-92)
Market Value: A–$215 B–N/E

359

Misty™
11" • Seal • #7431
Issued: 1998 • Current
Market Value: $_____

360

Mortimer™
18" • Moose • #7417
Issued: 1996 • Retired: 1998
Market Value: $25

361

Otto™
20" • Otter • #7417
Issued: 1993 • Retired: 1994
Market Value: $230

362

Patti™
20" • Panther • #1118
Issued: 1989 • Retired: 1990
A. No Ribbon (1990) B. Ribbon (1989)
Market Value: A/B–$1,000

263

Rascal™
16" • Monkey • #7001
Issued: 1994 • Retired: 1997
Market Value: $80

	Wildlife		
	Date Purchased	Price Paid	Value
357.			
358.			
359.			
360.			
361.			
362.			
363.			
Totals			

Ty Classic™

364

Sahara™
12" • Lion • #7421
Issued: 1995 • Current
A. Floppy/Gold Chest/Long Mane
(1998-Current)
B. Sitting/Gold Chest/Long Mane (1996)
C. Sitting/White Chest/Short Mane (1995)
Market Value: A–$_____ B–$63 C–$63

365

New!

Serengeti™
13" • Zebra • #7425
Issued: 2000 • Current
Market Value: $_____

366

Shivers™
9" • Penguin • #7419
Issued: 1993 • Retired: 1994
Market Value: $312

367

Spout™
9" • Elephant • #7426
Issued: 1996 • Current
A. Floppy (1998-Current)
B. Sitting (1996-97)
Market Value: A–$_____ B–$35

368

Super Chi-Chi™
52" • Cheetah • #9004
Issued: 1989 • Retired: 1989
Market Value: $1,100

369

Super George™
38" • Gorilla • #9007
Issued: 1990 • Retired: 1991
Market Value: $1,000

Wildlife

	Date Purchased	Price Paid	Value
364.			
365.			
366.			
367.			
368.			
369.			
Totals			

370

Super Jake™
16" • Monkey • #7002
Issued: 1988 • Retired: 1989
Market Value: $1,150

371

Super Jake™
N/A • Monkey • #7002B
Issued: 1989 • Retired: 1989
Market Value: N/E

372

Super Jake™
N/A • Monkey • #7002R
Issued: 1989 • Retired: 1989
Market Value: N/E

373

Super Jake™
55" • Monkey • #9001
Issued: 1989 • Retired: 1989
Market Value: $1,150

374

Super Tygger™
32" • Tiger • #9004
Issued: 1990 • Retired: 1991
Market Value: $1,000

375

Tango™
12" • Monkey • #7000
Issued: 1995 • Retired: 1998
Market Value: $24

376

Tango™
12" • Monkey • #7002
Issued: 1995 • Retired: 1998
Market Value: $22

Wildlife

	Date Purchased	Price Paid	Value
370.			
371.			
372.			
373.			
374.			
375.			
376.			
Totals			

377

Twiggy™
23" • Giraffe • #7422
Issued: 1991 • Retired: 1996
Market Value: $182

378

Tygger™
20" • Tiger • #1120
Issued: 1990 • Retired: 1990
Market Value: $800

379

Tygger™
20" • Tiger • #7420
Issued: 1991 • Retired: 1998
A. Floppy (1994-98)
B. Standing (1992-93)
C. Floppy (1991)
Market Value: A–$130 B–$232 C–N/E

380

Tygger™
20" • Tiger • #7421
Issued: 1991 • Retired: 1992
Market Value: $490

381

Wally™
12" • Walrus • #7423
Issued: 1992 • Retired: 1993
Market Value: $180

382

Zulu™
20" • Zebra • #7421
Issued: 1994 • Retired: 1994
Market Value: $375

Wildlife

	Date Purchased	Price Paid	Value
377.			
378.			
379.			
380.			
381.			
382.			
Totals			

Future Releases

Use this page to record future releases and purchases.

Ty® Plush Animals	Item #	Status	Price Paid	Market Value

Page Total:	Price Paid	Value

Total Value Of My Collection

Record the value of your collection here by adding the
pencil totals from the bottom of each Value Guide page.

Attic Treasures™

Page Number	Price Paid	Market Value
Page 33		
Page 34		
Page 35		
Page 36		
Page 37		
Page 38		
Page 39		
Page 40		
Page 41		
Page 42		
Page 43		
Page 44		
Page 45		
Page 46		
Page 47		
Page 48		
Page 49		
Page 50		
Page 51		
Page 52		
Page 53		
Page 54		
Page 55		
Page 56		
Page 57		
Page 58		
Page 59		
Page 60		
Page 61		
Page 62		
Page 63		
Subtotal		

Baby Ty™

Page Number	Price Paid	Market Value
Page 64		
Page 65		

Beanie Babies®

Page Number	Price Paid	Market Value
Page 66		
Page 67		
Page 68		
Page 69		
Page 70		
Page 71		
Page 72		
Page 73		
Page 74		
Page 75		
Page 76		
Page 77		
Page 78		
Page 79		
Page 80		
Page 81		
Page 82		
Page 83		
Page 84		
Page 85		
Page 86		
Page 87		
Page 88		
Page 89		
Page 90		
Page 91		
Page 92		
Page 93		
Page 94		
Subtotal		

Total Value Of My Collection

Record the value of your collection here by adding the
pencil totals from the bottom of each Value Guide page.

Beanie Babies®

Page Number	Price Paid	Market Value
Page 95		
Page 96		
Page 97		
Page 98		
Page 99		
Page 100		
Page 101		
Page 102		
Page 103		
Page 104		
Page 105		
Page 106		
Page 107		
Page 108		
Page 109		
Page 110		
Page 111		
Page 112		
Page 113		
Page 114		
Page 115		
Page 116		

Sports Promotions

Page Number	Price Paid	Market Value
Page 117		
Page 118		
Page 119		
Page 120		

Beanie Buddies®

Page Number	Price Paid	Market Value
Page 121		
Page 122		
Page 123		
Subtotal		

Beanie Buddies®

Page Number	Price Paid	Market Value
Page 124		
Page 125		
Page 126		
Page 127		
Page 128		
Page 129		
Page 130		
Page 131		
Page 132		
Page 133		
Page 134		
Page 135		
Page 136		

Teenie Beanie Babies™

Page Number	Price Paid	Market Value
Page 137		
Page 138		
Page 139		
Page 140		
Page 141		

Beanie Kids™

Page Number	Price Paid	Market Value
Page 142		
Page 143		
Page 144		

Pillow Pals®

Page Number	Price Paid	Market Value
Page 145		
Page 146		
Page 147		
Page 148		
Page 149		
Page 150		
Page 151		
Subtotal		

Total Value Of My Collection

Record the value of your collection here by adding the
pencil totals from the bottom of each Value Guide page.

Ty Classic™

Page Number	Price Paid	Market Value
Page 152		
Page 153		
Page 154		
Page 155		
Page 156		
Page 157		
Page 158		
Page 159		
Page 160		
Page 161		
Page 162		
Page 163		
Page 164		
Page 165		
Page 166		
Page 167		
Page 168		
Page 169		
Page 170		
Page 171		
Page 172		
Page 173		
Page 174		
Page 175		
Page 176		
Page 177		
Page 178		
Page 179		
Page 180		
Page 181		
Page 182		
Subtotal		

Ty Classic™

Page Number	Price Paid	Market Value
Page 183		
Page 184		
Page 185		
Page 186		
Page 187		
Page 188		
Page 189		
Page 190		
Page 191		
Page 192		
Page 193		
Page 194		
Page 195		
Page 196		
Page 197		
Page 198		
Page 199		
Page 200		
Page 201		
Page 202		
Page 203		
Page 204		
Page 205		
Page 206		
Page 207		
Page 208		
Page 209		
Page 210		
Subtotal		

Grand Total:	Price Paid	Value

Making The Secondary Market Work For You

If you didn't start collecting *Beanie Babies*, *Pillow Pals* or any of the other Ty plush lines from the very beginning, but you want to acquire the complete collection, you may find that tracking down those retired and older critters is not easy. If you're wondering how to get your hands on those elusive creatures that have retired and long since disappeared from retail store shelves, then this section is for you! Over the next few pages we'll give you a secondary market crash course, in which you'll learn how to find and purchase all those collectibles you've only dreamed of owning. Before you know it, your collection will be complete . . . and then it will be time to start on the next collection!

What Is The Secondary Market?

If you're new to collecting, you may not be familiar with the secondary market. The secondary market is the place where collectibles are bought and sold according to the laws of supply and demand. Pieces that are not readily available in retail stores, or that have sold out or been retired are often sold on the secondary market at prices higher than their original retail value. This is because the lower the supply of a particular item, the greater the demand for it, which means that consumers are generally willing to pay higher prices to acquire that item.

In the olden days, collectors in search of retired or rare pieces often had to travel to swap meets, flea markets and tag sales, or scour the classified ads in their local papers in the hopes of finding someone selling the item that they wanted to buy. While those means can work – and nothing can beat the thrill of finding some long sought-after item sitting innocently on a card table at a neighborhood garage sale for 25 cents – there is another resource literally at your fingertips that can put you in touch with collectors all over the globe!

Introducing The Internet

Over the last few years, the Internet has emerged as one of the easiest, quickest and most popular way to buy and sell collectibles on the secondary market. A host of on-line auction sites has sprung up all over the Internet, and many have thousands of listings in every possible category of collectible. Looking for a Royal Blue Peanut *Beanie Baby?* Simply type key words such as "Beanie Baby," "Retired Beanie Babies," or even "Peanut Beanie Baby" into an auction search engine, and you're off and running! It's usually possible to find even the rarest Ty collectibles on Internet auction sites.

Of course, the fun doesn't stop at auctions! There are a great number of on-line retail stores that deal in rare and retired collectibles. Consider also hopping on a message board or trading post at one of the many unofficial web sites devoted to Ty products. You'll  be sure to find many like-minded collectors who can help you in your quest. You may even make some new friends!

But before you bid on or purchase that hard-to-find piece, there are a few things that you should keep in mind.

Buyer Beware!

If you are participating in an on-line auction, it's always wise to decide in advance how much you are willing to spend for a particular item. It's easy to get caught up in the moment and end up bidding too much money for something that is, after all, only a stuffed toy. Remember, collecting is a fun hobby — it shouldn't drive you into debt.

Let's say you've studied your *Collector's Value Guide*, decided what you are willing to spend and won the auction or decided to purchase a piece from a dealer for a reasonable price. Now what? It's always a good idea to check out the reputation of the seller before any money changes hands. Most auction sites have a feedback area where collectors can leave comments about their experiences with various sellers (and buyers). If there are many negative comments about a certain seller, he or she is probably not someone whom you want to do business with. If you're buying from a dealer, it might be wise to obtain additional information about him or her business practices from the Better Business Bureau (*www.BBBonline.org*).

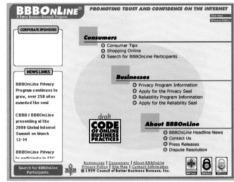

It's also in your best interest to only buy items that the sellers have provided pictures of; that way, you know exactly what you're buying. If it's not possible to see a photo, at least make sure that the seller provides a detailed, written description. If you have questions about the item, don't hesitate to contact the seller via E-mail.

Also, familiarize yourself with the terms that are used to describe items for sale. Ty plush collectors have their own lingo to describe the condition of the pieces they are selling. Collectors are generally only willing to pay top dollar for items that have their swing tags still attached and in good condition. The highest rating a *Beanie Baby* or other Ty collectible can garner is MWMT, or "mint with mint tags." This means that the piece is not only as pristine as the day it was purchased, but also that the swing and tush tags are in near-perfect condition as well. For the swing tag to be considered mint, it should have no creases, tears or any other imperfection. There is more leeway with tush tags. As long as a tush tag is readable, it is generally considered to be in mint condition. "Mint with creased tag," or "MWCT," means just that — the item itself is in perfect condition, but the swing tag is creased. As a general rule, prices listed in value guides such as this one are for pieces that are mint with mint tags.

Catching The Counterfeits

Savvy shoppers should also familiarize themselves with the traits of counterfeit Ty plush toys before purchasing anything on the secondary market. There are several ways to spot a counterfeit. The swing tags can often be a tell-tale sign of a fake. Swing tags should not have smeared ink, jagged edges, uneven gold foil around the front of the heart or errors in spelling or punctuation. They should also be a uniform size. Another way to spot an imposter is by inspecting the stitching. Fake Ty plush animals may have uneven or messy stitching. Look also at the colors of the toy. Do they bleed or look dyed? If so, it's probably a fake. The easiest way to spot a counterfeit is to compare it against the real thing. When going to shows or flea markets, bring along a genuine *Beanie Baby* or other Ty plush product for comparison. If you have suspicions about an item's authenticity, it's always better to be safe and not buy it than sorry that you did buy it.

Now that you have the know-how, get out there and start bidding! Remember that the guidelines discussed in this section also apply to other secondary marketplaces. Don't be afraid to ask questions of the seller, and always make sure that you are getting what you pay for. After all, without collectors like you, there would be no such thing as a secondary market.

Variations

Part of the fun of collecting Ty products is searching for the variations, or changes, that may occur in individual pieces. These variations, such as color, design or name changes, can be due to human error or the whim of the manufacturer, and range from the very subtle to the quite dramatic.

Some variations, especially rare ones, can command extremely high prices on the secondary market. Others are valuable only as a conversation piece or point of interest. It's often difficult to predict just what effect a specific variation may have on the value of a piece, so it's important to realize that the fun of searching for and acquiring such a piece may be your only reward. With that said, there are certain variations that can enhance the value of a piece.

Wardrobe

Let's start with the characters in the *Attic Treasures* line, who are infamous for playing tricks on those who collect them. Often, *Attic Treasures* will pop up sporting different outfits, or even going from "bare" to fashionably clad.

"Checkers" the panda is one such example. He first appeared undressed, but after a year he put on a vest. He must have tired of wearing the same old thing every day, though, because after a year he then went back to his old "bare" self. "Sara" the hare, on the other hand, went quite the other way. She first wore only a ribbon, but apparently felt it didn't do her beauty justice, for she later appeared wearing lovely pink bloomers.

The characters in the *Ty Classic* line are no different. "Snowball" went from no ribbon to a blue ribbon before finally deciding he looked best in a red ribbon.

Changes in clothing will sometimes command a higher secondary market value, though it is generally not because of the costume changes, but rather because the first design produced of a given piece is generally more highly coveted. Exercise caution when purchasing pieces of this kind on the secondary market. Remember, it's not difficult to undress a plush piece currently produced with clothing to make it appear to be an earlier "bare" version. Always check the generation of the swing and tush tags to see if they match the style of the piece (for more information on swing and tush tags, see pages 224-232).

Changes In Color

Color changes among members of the Ty family also tend to generate interest among collectors. One of the most talked about color variations is the case of the *Beanie Babies* "Iggy" and "Rainbow." After a few months of production, these two reptiles switched coats, with the result that "Iggy" now sports a blue hue, while "Rainbow" is now – appropriately – "Ty" dyed.

Another *Beanie Baby*, "Peanut," also had a change of heart with regard to color. After a short production run as a royal blue elephant, he decided to lighten up a little, and soon appeared in a light blue shade. Interestingly, his *Beanie Buddy* cousin also experienced some color confusion. "Peanut" the *Beanie Buddy* was primarily produced in royal blue, but has been spotted from time to time wearing a light blue coat.

"Digger" the *Beanie Baby* must have been feeling crabby about being orange, because after a year he turned red, significantly raising the value of the orange "Digger."

Over in *Ty Classic* land, a cow named "Jersey" decided to stand out from the crowd by changing her brown and white fur to black and white. And some animals just can't decide which color suits them best. "Mischief" the monkey went from white, to auburn, to white again during his six-year production run.

One of the more subtle variations is when an animal undergoes a change in its stitching. These alterations often go unnoticed, but keen eyes are rewarded, for they often command a higher value on the secondary market. One such case is the *Beanie Baby* "Magic," who has sported various shades of pink thread in her stitching.

Design Differences

Although color changes are certainly very dramatic, design changes can also be exciting. Often, though, collectors may not realize that a piece that has been redesigned is technically still the same piece. While design changes often bring about the complete physical overhaul of a piece, its style number and name generally remain the same.

One of the most obvious cases of this sort of variation can be seen with the "old face" and "new face" versions of the "Teddy" *Beanie Babies*. These were originally produced with pointed snouts and widely spaced eyes, but were redesigned with rounded faces and closer-set eyes.

Design changes aren't confined just to the *Beanie Baby* family, however. In 1996, a *Ty Classic* rabbit named "Peter" suddenly improved his hopping skills when he acquired jointed limbs. He also became more realistic looking, with changes to his face and ears. "Bengal" the tiger loosened up a little and went from a fairly rigid sitting position to a floppy pose, while "Elmer" the elephant must have had a growth spurt, because his trunk grew longer. And *Ty Classic* cats such as "Al E. Kat" and "Maggie" have gone from lying flat on their bellies to a cozier, curled-up position.

Some design changes don't affect the piece itself, but rather an aspect of it. "Sterling," the *Attic Treasure* angel bear, was originally released with very large wings. But they must have been getting in the way, because he later appeared with significantly smaller wings.

Sometimes certain animals get tired of the skin they're in, so to speak, and decide to alter their coat, mane or whiskers. The *Beanie Baby* "Inch" is an example of the latter case. He made the transition from felt to yarn antennas after several months of production. "Mystic" the unicorn went through a couple of mane changes before finally settling an a fluffy mane, as did his buddy "Derby."

The Name Game

In keeping with the old adage, "A rose by any other name would smell as sweet," several Ty plush pieces have undergone name changes.

One of the more valuable name changes occurred in the *Beanie Babies* line. "Bongo" the monkey was originally known as "Nana." Currently, "Nana" is worth several thousand dollars more on the secondary market than her "Bongo" counterpart. "Brownie," whose name was changed to "Cubbie," is also more valuable with his original moniker. It's important to note, however, that not all name changes result in increased value for the original.

Nana ™ style 4067

to _____

from _____
with
love

Bongo ™ style 4067

to _____

from _____
with
love

Sometimes what appears to be a name change is simply a swing tag error. For example, the *Ty Classic* critter "Baby Spice" sometimes sports a tag reading "ByBy Spice," and the *Beanie Baby* "Spooky" has occasionally turned up with a highly valuable "Spook" tag. Other times, a swing tag (or tush tag) might actually belong to another member of the family, as in the famous case of the switched tags of the *Beanie Babies* "Echo" and "Waves."

Recently, a widespread tag typo occurred involving the misspelling of "Millennium" on the *Beanie Baby* of the same name. This bear first sported a "Millenium" swing and tush tag. The error was then corrected on

Millenium ™

DATE OF BIRTH: January 1, 1999

A brand new century has come to call
Health and happiness to one and all
Bring on the fireworks and all the fun
Let's keep the party going 'til 2001 !

www.ty.com

Millennium ™

OF BIRTH: January 1, 1999

A brand new century has come to call
Health and happiness to one and all
ring on the fireworks and all the fun
's keep the party going 'til 2001 !

www.ty.com

the tush tag, but not the swing tag. Eventually, the error was corrected on both tags. Other errors can sometimes pop up on swing tags, as well. It's not uncommon to find words in the *Beanie Babies* poems misspelled, or other typos such as "Suface Wash" instead of "Surface Wash." In most cases, these types of errors do not generally result in a significant value difference over the correct versions.

Does Size Matter?

Another type of variation occurs when an animal has a sudden growth (or shrinking) spurt. This is not uncommon in the *Ty Classic* line. For the first year of his life, "Curly" the bear measured 22 inches. By the next year, he had shrunk to 18 inches, a height he has since maintained. "Kasey" the koala, on the other hand, must have been eating her Wheaties, because she grew a full 7 inches, from 13 inches in 1989 to 20 inches in 1990. She also changed colors, going from brown to a more realistic gray.

Given the number of variations in the Ty plush world, it is nearly impossible to keep track of them all, or to predict which ones will command higher prices on the secondary market. The fun of the variations is just knowing they are out there, and keeping your eyes peeled to spot one. Looking for variations can add a whole other dimension to collecting, and while finding one with a high value is definitely great, collectors should never lose sight of the fact that collecting is really all about having fun.

Swing Tags

The heart swing tags of the Ty plush animals are one of the primary means of determining secondary market value for Ty products, which mark tag "generations." Generally, Ty plush animals with earlier tags are more valuable than animals with later tags.

Attic Treasures™

Generation 1: The first *Attic Treasures* tags have the word "ty" printed on the front in a skinny font, and "ty" and the heart are outlined in gold. The tag's back contains the name of the collection, the animal and the designer, as well as the style number, cleaning instructions and the piece's production location. The company address is also noted.

The Attic Treasures Collection
Emily ™ . Style 6016
© 1992 Ty Inc. Oakbrook, IL USA
Designed by: Nola Hart
All Rights Reserved. Caution:
Remove this tag before giving
toy to a child. For ages 5 and up.
Printed in Korea.
Handmade in China.
Surface
Wash

Generation 2: This tag opens like a book. Inside, the collection name, company information and care instructions are on the left. On the right is "to/from/with love" below the animal's name and style number.

The Attic Treasures Collection
© 1993 Ty Inc. Oakbrook IL. USA
All Rights Reserved, Caution:
Remove this tag before giving
toy to a child. For ages 3 and up.
Handmade in China
Surface
Wash.

Cassie ™ style 6028
to _____
from _____
with
love

Generation 3: This style appeared only for a brief time. The skinny font on the front is replaced by the fatter letters still in use today.

The Attic Treasures Collection
© 1993 Ty Inc. Oakbrook IL. USA
All Rights Reserved, Caution:
Remove this tag before giving
toy to a child. For ages 3 and up.
Handmade in China
Surface
Wash.

Emily ™ style 6018
to _____
from _____
with
love

Generation 4: A green stripe with the word "COLLECTIBLE" appears diagonally across the upper right-hand corner of this tag. Inside are the addresses of Ty's corporate locations, as well as the name of the collection, which is now called "Ty Collectibles™." Information on care and caution has been moved to the tag's reverse.

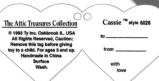

Ty Collectibles ™
©Ty Inc.
Oakbrook IL. U.S.A.
Ty UK Ltd.
Waterlooville, Hants
PO8 8HH
Ty Deutschland
90008 Nürnberg
Handmade in China

Jeremy ™ style 6008
to _____
from _____
with
love

Generation 5: The front of the tag is now beige and covered with brown paw prints. The gold trim is gone, and the logo and the "collectible" banner are now burgundy. The information inside the tag remains the same, but an additional safety warning has been added to the back of the tag.

Generation 6: This tag gives the name of the collection as either "The Attic Treasures Collection" or "Ty Collectibles." The style number has moved from the inside to the back, appearing as the last four numbers of the UPC code. "Buttons" has been removed from the safety precautions.

Generation 7: It's back to the familiar gold-trimmed red and white tag. The information on the inside left is the same, but the right side now lists the animal's name, followed by a short phrase regarding its personality. At the bottom is Ty Inc.'s web address. Some later tags have a change in the way the corporate information is listed. It has been truncated to Ty Inc., Ty Canada, Ty Europe and Ty Japan.

Baby Ty™

The outside of the the Baby Ty tag has the white Ty logo, and the heart is trimmed in gold. In the upper right-hand corner the word "Baby" is spelled out in pastel-colored blocks. The left side lists the name of the collection as "The Pillow Pals Collection®," and the Ty corporate locations follow. The inside right features the name of the animal and the official Ty web address.

Beanie Babies®

Generation 1 (Early 1994 - Mid 1994): The first *Beanie Babies* had a red heart-shaped, single-sheet swing tag. The Ty logo is printed on the front in a skinny font. The logo and the outer edge of the tag are trimmed in gold. On the reverse is the *Beanie Baby's* name and style number along with "The Beanie Babies Collection" and copyright and safety information.

The Beanie Babies Collection
Brownie ™ style 4010
© 1993 Ty Inc. Oakbrook, IL. USA
All Rights Reserved. Caution:
Remove this tag before giving
toy to a child. For ages 5 and up.
Handmade in Korea.
Surface
Wash.

Generation 2 (Mid 1994 - Early 1995): This tag opens like a book. The name of the collection, company information, care instructions and cautions are on the left of the tag, while the right features the name and style number of the *Beanie Baby* along with "to ____ /from ____/with love."

The Beanie Babies Collection
© 1993 Ty Inc. Oakbrook IL. USA
All Rights Reserved, Caution:
Remove this tag before giving
toy to a child. For ages 3 and up.
Handmade in China
Surface
Wash.

Chilly ™ style 4012
to ____
from ____
with
love

Generation 3 (Early 1995 - Early 1996): On this tag, the Ty logo letters are fat and puffy. The inside left of the tag says "The Beanie Babies" Collection," and lists Ty's three corporate addresses.

The Beanie Babies ™ Collection
℗ Ty Inc.
Oakbrook, IL. U.S.A.
℗ Ty UK Ltd.
Waterlooville, Hants
PO8 8HH
℗ Ty Deutschland
90008 Nürnberg
Handmade in China

Garcia ™ style 4051
to ____
from ____
with
love

Generation 4 (Early 1996 - Late 1997): A yellow star with the words "Original Beanie Baby" is on the front in the upper right-hand corner. The Ty logo is no longer trimmed in gold, and the "y" in Ty is moved down a little to make room for the star. Inside, the "to/from" section is replaced with the *Beanie Baby's* birthday and poem, and "Visit our web page!!!" appears above the Ty web address.

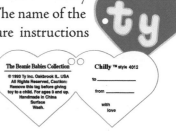

Generation 5 (Late 1997 - Late 1999): The typeface of "Original Beanie Baby" and the inside text is changed, the *Beanie Baby's* birthday is written out, "Visit our web page!!!" is removed, and the web address is shortened. Additionally, the *Beanie*

The Beanie Babies™Collection
℗ Ty Inc.
Oakbrook IL. U.S.A.
℗ Ty UK Ltd.
Fareham, Hants
PO15 5TX
℗ Ty Deutschland
90008 Nürnberg
Handmade in China

Doodle™ style 4171
DATE OF BIRTH : 3 - 8 - 96
Listen closely to "cock-a-doodle-doo"
What's the rooster saying to you?
Hurry, wake up sleepy head
We have lots to do, get out of bed!
Visit our web page!!!
http://www.ty.com

Baby's style number is moved to the last four digits of the UPC bar code on the back. "The Beanie Babies Collection" now has a registration mark. The corporate offices overseas are now "Ty Europe."

In the summer of 1998, there were reports of variations. The writing in the star is in a different font, and the writing on the inside and back of the tag is larger and darker. The Ty Europe Ltd. address is now "Gasport, Hampshire, U.K."

Generation 6 (Early 2000 - Current): A flashy, iridescent silver star adorns the upper-right corner of the tag. Splashed across the star is "2000" written in yellow. On the inside, the Ty corporate office addresses are shortened.

Beanie Buddies®

Generation 1 (1998 - Late 1999): The outside of this tag looks like a *Beanie Babies* Generation 5 swing tag (with the word "Buddy" in the star). The Ty Europe Ltd. address on the inside left as Fareham, Hants was changed to "Gasport, Hampshire, U.K." This was again changed to the correct spelling of Gosport. The right side lists the animal's name and a fact about its *Beanie Baby* counterpart, as well as the official Ty web address.

Generation 2 (Early 2000 - Current): The star on this tag is in tie-dyed colors. The corporate addresses on the inside left of the tag are listed as Ty Inc., Ty Canada, Ty Europe and Ty Japan.

Teenie Beanie Babies™

1997 Version: These tags are a single sheet and feature the red, gold and white front design with the puffy Ty logo. On the reverse is the name of the collection and the animal, as well as company information.

Teenie Beanie Babies™
Patti™ ©Ty Inc.
Oakbrook, IL

Printed in China
Imprimé en Chine

1998 Version: The official Ty web address has been added to the back of the tag. The trademark symbols read "TM/MC/MR," and a different font is used on all of the type.

TM/MC/MR
Teenie Beanie Babies
Bongo ©Ty Inc.
Oakbrook, IL

www.ty.com
Printed in China
Imprimé en Chine

1999 Version: The 1999 tags are larger than their predecessors. On the front, the Ty logo is no longer gold-trimmed, and a yellow star with "Original Teenie Beanie" has been added. The font on the reverse of the tag has been changed yet again, and the animal type has been added after each *Teenie Beanies'* name. The trademark symbol is simply "TM."

Teenie Beanie Babies™
Stretchy ©Ty Inc.
the Ostrich™ Oakbrook, IL

www.ty.com
Printed in China
Imprimé en Chine

Beanie Kids™

The *Beanie Kids* swing tag is the familiar red heart with the "ty" logo in white. The heart is bordered in gold, with "Beanie Kids" printed in the upper-right corner in multi-colored, child-like letters. On the inside, "The Beanie Kids Collection™" and the locations of Ty Inc.'s corporate offices are listed on the left, while the right side lists the *Beanie Kid's* name and a trademark symbol. Beneath the name is the date of birth and a short poem, followed by the Ty web address.

The Beanie Kids Collection™ Chipper™

® Ty Inc. DATE OF BIRTH: July 20, 1997
® Ty Canada Happy and cheerful, big hugs for all,
® Ty Europe smiling and laughing - life is a ball !
® Ty Japan
  www.ty.com
Handmade in China

Pillow Pals®

Pillow Pals have large, red, heart-shaped tags and the puffy Ty logo, both outlined in gold. The tag opens like a book with "The Pillow Pals Collection," and company and age suitability information on the inside left. The right side lists the piece's name and its style number above the "to/from/with love" section. Later, a smaller tag was introduced that included the care and age suitability information on the back. A subsequent design features a different font, and the piece's style number has moved from the inside to the back as the last four numbers of the UPC bar code. In 1998, a new tag design appeared that replaced the "to/from/with love" section with prayer poems.

The Pillow Pals Collection®

© Ty Inc.
Oakbrook, IL. U.S.A.

© Ty Europe Ltd.
Fareham, Hants
PO15 5TX, U.K.

© Ty Canada
Aurora, Ontario
Handmade in China

Sherbet™

Dear God, be with me as I start my day,
Please watch over me during school and play.

www.ty.com

The Pillow Pals Collection®

© Ty Inc.
Oakbrook, IL. U.S.A.

© Ty Europe
Gosport, Hampshire, U.K.

© Ty Canada
Aurora, Ontario
Handmade in China

Meow™

As the day ends and turns to night,
Thank you God, for each twinkling light.

www.ty.com

Ty Classic™

When the line was first introduced in 1986, a red plastic heart tag was attached to the animal's neck. Several versions of the heart-shaped paper tag followed. Some tags only show the Ty logo, while others have "BEAN BAG" in red letters on a diagonal yellow banner in the upper right-hand corner. On later versions, the Ty logo appears horizontally with the letters "t" and "y" used as the first letters for the words "to" and "you," and the words "with love" written in script. Sometimes the tag design mirrors the original Ty logo, but has a black border around the letters. The tag design later changed to the "puffed out" Ty logo. The most recent tags feature the word "Classic" written in gold on the front and the Ty corporate addresses on the inside left of the tag. Two tag sizes are used, depending on the size of the animal to which it is attached.

© Ty Inc.

© Ty Canada

© Ty Europe

© Ty Japan

Handmade in China

Scooter™

to _____
from _____
with
love

Tush Tags

The cloth tags sewn into the seam on the back of Ty products have also seen changes. Although the information on these tags can be useful to determine the value and age of a particular piece, it is not the most accurate way to do so. It's not uncommon to find a new piece with an older date on the tag.

Attic Treasures™

The first *Attic Treasures* tush tags are white with black printing and no Ty logo. The next tag design features a white tag with the Ty heart logo and red printing. Currently, the *Attic Treasures* tag is burgundy with the "ty" logo inside a white heart on the front, with cleaning instructions and company and content information on the reverse in white print. All of the writing is embroidered.

Baby Ty™

The *Baby Ty* tush tags are white with the red heart "ty" logo and the words "100% Tylon" on the front and company and cleaning information on the back.

Beanie Babies®

Version 1: The first *Beanie Babies* tush tag is white with black printing. It lists production and company information, as well as the material used and age recommendations.

© 1993 TY INC., OAKBROOK, IL, U.S.A. ALL RIGHTS RESERVED HAND MADE IN CHINA SURFACE WASHABLE	ALL NEW MATERIAL POLYESTER FIBER & P.V.C. PELLETS PA. REG #1965 FOR AGES 3 AND UP

Version 1

Version 2   **Version 3**

Version 2: The Ty logo appears inside a red heart and the text is now printed in red. The tag reads vertically.

Version 3: "The Beanie Babies Collection™" is printed above a small red Ty heart logo and the name of the animal is written beneath it. The company information remains the same, but the age recommendations have changed.

Version 4   **Version 5**

Version 4:   On this tag a tiny red star appears to the upper left of the Ty heart logo. In some cases, a clear sticker with the star is placed next to the Ty logo.

Version 5:   A registration mark appears after the collection's name and a trademark symbol appears after the animal's name.

Version 6:   The registration mark in the collection's name moves and some of the tags note a change from "P.V.C." to "P.E" pellets.   In mid-1998, an oval red stamp containing numbers and Chinese characters begins appearing inside the loop on some tags.

Version 7:   A hologram bearing the name of the collection appears on this tag and a red heart is printed on the back in disappearing ink.

Version 6   **Version 7**

Version 8

Version 8:   The hologram tags now appear as a single flap rather than looped.   The hologram and name are on the front and the remaining information is on the back.

Beanie Buddies®

Version 1:   These tags are white with an embroidered red heart with the Ty logo inside in white letters.   On the reverse, company and fabric information are embroidered in black. *Note: tag in photo is unfolded.*

Version 1   **Version 2**

Version 2:   "The Beanie Buddies Collection®" is printed on the front of this tush tag above the heart.   The back remains the same except that the text is written in red. *Note: tag in photo is unfolded.*

Version 3

Version 3:   This tag looks like Version 2 except for the addition of "Shell 100% Tylon" on the front, and "Inner Contents" on the back. *Note: tag in photo is unfolded.*

Teenie Beanie Babies™

These tags feature the red heart logo, company and production information, and the copyright date printed in red ink. The 1999 tags have a large, fat "ty" logo. The tag's reverse is printed in black ink. There are small differences among tags with regard to content information and the McDonald's corporate name.

Beanie Kids™

The *Beanie Kids'* tag is similar to the Version 8 *Beanie Babies* tag. It is white with a hologram on the front. The piece's name is below the hologram. Stamped on the inside is an eight-digit identification number. The tag's back features a heart that disappears when touched.

Ginger™

Pillow Pals®

The *Pillow Pals* tags originated with the red heart on the front and Ty company information, age and care recommendations on the back. Over time, the information concerning age was deleted and the "CE" symbol was added.

Ty Classic™

Tush tags are sometimes the only way to identify older stuffed animals that belong to the Ty collection, especially those that have lost their swing tags. There have been several different versions of *Ty Classic* tush tags. One of the early versions is white satin with a red heart outline surrounding the word "ty," which is written in black. A later tag features the red Ty heart logo on the front of a white tag, with "Ty, Inc." and the copyright year printed in red on the reverse and company and production information printed in black or dark brown type. The information regarding the pellets and the country of production varies.

Protecting And Insuring Your Collection

Whether you're a first-time collector or an avid secondary market enthusiast, consideration should always be given to the care, cleaning and insuring of your Ty collectibles. Keeping your animal in tip-top shape (and retaining its value) requires time, tenacity and perhaps a talk with your insurance agent!

1. Where There's Smoke . . . Many "for sale" listings often reference "from a smoke-free home," so you should always be sure to keep your collectibles . . . ahem . . . out of the line of fire. Whether it be from cigarettes, cooking, or even a fireplace, smoke adheres to the soft fur of your animals and will linger long after the odor is out of the house. To ensure a fresh smell, always keep your collectibles safely away from any olfactory offenders. You can protect your collection from unpleasant odors by placing your pieces in acrylic storage boxes available in stores. Aside from protecting your animals from smells, these boxes provide another way to store and display your collection. You can also choose to keep your pieces in airtight plastic bags purchased from your local grocery store.

2. Calgon Take Me Away . . . Though Ty products are built to withstand all the love and attention they deserve, there is often little you can do to prevent dirt from making its way onto your beloved animals. Therefore, when stains appear, consider a rub in the tub for your favorite friend.

Intended for use by tiny tots, Ty's *Baby Ty*, *Beanie Babies* and *Pillow Pals* are machine washable. Before bathtime, however, be sure to check for any fabric held on by glue. If your animal has felt spots, for example, you may be better off proceeding with a surface washing. If all systems are go for a ride in the rinse cycle, there are a couple of simple steps to follow. Being sure to remove the swing tag, place the animal inside a pillow case and secure the opening with a shoestring. Use a mild detergent and your machine's gentle cycle.

Finally, either let your animal air dry or fluff with a hair dryer on a cool setting.

To clean other Ty Plush products, it is best to "surface wash." Simply place a mild detergent on a damp washcloth and begin by testing a hidden area of the animal's coat to ensure that the fabric will maintain its color and quality. Once the area has dried and you can tell that no damage has been done, remove dirt by rubbing the fabric carefully until the stain is lifted.

3. Tending To Tags ... Keeping Ty tags in tip-top shape should be a top priority for any collector. You'll often find that wrinkled or ripped tags will dramatically decrease the value of your collectible. Therefore, you should be sure to protect your tags by encasing them in clear acrylic tag protectors available in  stores. You may want to consider the added protection of buying a tag protector that is UV coated, as the sun causes tags to fade from their vibrant red color to soft pink.

4. Investigate Insurance . . . As with any of the valuables in your home, make sure your Ty collectibles are fully insured. Though Ty products are marketed as children's toys, with their increasing values you want to be prepared if accidents happen. While most renter's or homeowner's insurance policies cover collectibles, you should check with your agent to ensure that coverage is at current replacement value. If you find that you need additional coverage for your collection, consider taking out a personal articles or fine arts floater or rider, so that you have adequate insurance.

To prepare yourself in the event of an emergency, always keep an accurate record of your collection on hand, including receipts and dates of purchase. Consider photographing your pieces (including tags); this way, if you need to make a claim against your policy, you will have the specifics of your collection, such as variations and the generation tags. Also be sure to keep copies of your *Collector's Value Guide™ To Ty® Plush Animals* in a safe deposit box or another safe location so you can access the value of your collection at any time.

Glossary

CE – mark imprinted on tush tags, indicating that the pieces were manufactured according to consumer safety regulations.

Collectible – anything that is "able to be collected. However, it is generally recognized that a true collectible should be something that increases in value.

Current – a piece that is in production and available in stores.

Mint Condition – a piece offered on the secondary market that is in like-new condition. It may also be stated as "MWMT," which means the piece, as well as both of its tags, are in perfect, or like-new, condition.

Mint In Bag (**MIB**) – on the secondary market, the term used for *Teenie Beanie Babies* in like-new condition, still in their original, unopened plastic bags.

P.E. Pellets – small, round plastic polyethylene "beans" used as weighted fillings in many Ty plush animals.

P.V.C. Pellets – small round plastic polyvinyl chloride "beans" used as weighted fillings in many Ty plush animals.

Retired – a piece that is taken out of production.

Secondary Market – the source for buying and selling collectibles according to basic supply-and-demand principles. Popular pieces can appreciate in value far above their original issue prices.

Tag Generation – style changes in the swing tags, which can help determine the approximate age of Ty plush animals.

Tylon – a special fabric developed by Ty Warner. This fabric is very soft and cool to the touch.

Variation – an item that has color, design or printed text changes from the "original" piece, whether intentional or not.

All Ty plush animals are listed below in alphabetical order. The first number refers to the piece's page location in the book and the second refers to the picture box in which it is shown on that page.

Alphabetical Index

Alphabetical Index

Alphabetical Index

Alphabetical Index